Herbert Schiller

CRITICAL MEDIA STUDIES
INSTITUTIONS, POLITICS, AND CULTURE

Series Editor
Andrew Calabrese, University of Colorado

Advisory Board

Recent Titles in the Series

Critical Communication Theory: Power, Media, Gender, and Technology,
 Sue Curry Jansen
Digital Disability: The Social Construction of Disability in New Media,
 Gerard Goggin and Christopher Newell
Principles of Publicity and Press Freedom,
 Slavko Splichal
Internet Governance in Transition: Who Is the Master of This Domain?
 Daniel J. Paré
Recovering a Public Vision for Public Television,
 Glenda R. Balas
Reality TV: The Work of Being Watched,
 Mark Andrejevic
Contesting Media Power: Alternative Media in a Networked World,
 edited by Nick Couldry and James Curran
Herbert Schiller,
 Richard Maxwell
Harold Innis,
 Paul Heyer

Forthcoming in the Series

Toward a Political Economy of Culture: Capitalism and Communication in the Twenty-First Century,
 edited by Andrew Calabrese and Colin Sparks
Public Service Broadcasting in Italy,
 Cinzia Padovani
Changing Concepts of Time,
 Harold A. Innis
Many Voices, One World,
 Seán MacBride
Film Industries and Cultures in Transition,
 Dina Iordanova
Globalizing Political Communication,
 Gerald Sussman
The Blame Game: Why Television Is Not Our Fault,
 Eileen R. Meehan
Mass Communication and Social Thought,
 edited by John Durham Peters and Peter Simonson
Entertaining the Citizen: When Politics and Popular Culture Converge,
 Liesbet van Zoonen
Elusive Autonomy: Brazilian Communications Policy,
 Sergio Euclides de Souza

Herbert Schiller

Richard Maxwell

ROWMAN & LITTLEFIELD PUBLISHERS, INC.
Lanham • Boulder • New York • Toronto • Oxford

ROWMAN & LITTLEFIELD PUBLISHERS, INC.

Published in the United States of America
by Rowman & Littlefield Publishers, Inc.
A wholly owned subsidiary of The Rowman & Littlefield Publishing Group, Inc.
4501 Forbes Boulevard, Suite 200, Lanham, MD 20706
www.rowmanlittlefield.com

P.O. Box 317, Oxford OX2 9RU, UK

Photographs in chapters 1, 4, 5, and the conclusion appear courtesy of Anita Schiller.

British Library Cataloguing in Publication Information Available

Library of Congress Cataloging-in-Publication Data

Maxwell, Richard, 1957–
    Herbert Schiller / Richard Maxwell.
        p.   cm. — (Critical media studies)
    Includes bibliographical references and index.
    ISBN 0-7425-1847-7 (cloth : alk. paper) — ISBN 0-7425-1848-5 (pbk. : alk. paper)
        1. Schiller, Herbert I., 1919–   2. Communication—United States.   3. Mass media—United States. I. Title. II. Series.
    P92.5.S35M39   2003
    302.2'092—dc21   2003009737

Printed in the United States of America

♾ ™ The paper used in this publication meets the minimum requirements of American National Standard for Information Sciences—Permanence of Paper for Printed Library Materials, ANSI/NISO Z39.48-1992.

For Luke

Contents

Preface

A book such as this one begins with a familiar story. There are teachers who inspire students to think critically and speak out against the injustices of the established order. They don't see any other way to live their life. Their spirited words stick with those few students who find a voice to challenge a society in which wealth dictates power and a mix of libertarian rage and privatized satisfaction define the common mode of personal survival. In American society, there are few rewards for unorthodox thinking or radical politics, yet the teachers who "touched our lives" seemed fulfilled and invariably hopeful that change would come about. They were the ones who taught us to be our best. They were the ones who helped us transcend the provincial life of the family and showed us ways to navigate through a perplexing world. They were the ones who helped us value the work of thought over the depressing thought of work alienated from anything that meant anything to us. As we listened to them speak, we took notes and wondered how they managed to recall such detail and come up with such ideas without any written script. They were funny, brilliant, scary. They didn't know it, of course. We rarely had the courage to tell them, but occasionally they would find out. A letter would arrive from a former student, from decades past, recalling a day long ago when a young man or woman went into a classroom unsure of what to expect and encountered a teacher whose ideas would make a positive difference in their life. This book is my letter to one of those teachers.

Students of media and communication will see the name Herbert I. Schiller cited routinely in their textbooks. That was his textual identity, the "I" for Irving worn like a tie to a meeting with the boss, the name he signed to his writing—H.I.S. They will learn that Schiller was a central figure in media and communication studies, though one hardly embraced by the majority of communication researchers. They may get a vague idea that his "status" as a key thinker and writer in the field had something to do with his political convictions. If assigned to read one of Schiller's major works, they would probably be unsettled by his unyielding criticism of the U.S. media and information industries. After all, most students major in communications and media studies as a way to get into the business, not to learn how to change it. Schiller would not have been surprised by this conservative attitude; nor would he have let it stop him from encouraging his students to question the current state of world affairs while making a career for themselves. He would simply have persisted in his explanations, hoping students learn a little more about what it takes to read and write from outside the mainstream.

This book aims to synthesize Schiller's work for a new generation of media and communications students and provide a sustained look at his work and career. In writing my version of Schiller's story, I began to consider how Herb Schiller became a politically engaged thinker before becoming Herbert I. Schiller, a founding figure of critical communication studies. I have tried to evoke the radical spirit and energy that motivated Schiller throughout his life and led to him becoming, in Edward Herman's (2002, 2) words, "the most original and influential media analyst of the left in the past half century." Schiller was a tireless correspondent, a political activist and public intellectual on an international scale; he was also a charmer, a humorist, a raconteur who endeavored throughout his life to represent the side of the have-nots of the world. He loved to take walks—more like street-level colloquia—in which ideas were bantered about at a pace set by the rhythm of his brisk, stretching stride, his perspicacity pulling his companions into a conversation that became more spirited and involving at every turn in the road. He was a marvelous public speaker with a talent for assessing the state of the mass media and connecting all the dots between who owned the media, who ruled the world, and why the two groups agreed on what was to be attempted. Schiller expressed his intellect and politics freely, the effect on thinking a liberating one. His style, by turns both elegant and pithy, never failed to be provocative; the effect could be exhilarating, an agitation to action, a prod to consciousness, as he might have said. His subjects included science and technology, human communication, politics and economics, but his ideas never got swamped in technical or academic jargon; the effect could be revelatory of that which the powers-that-be wished to obscure.

Much of the book is based on the autobiographical accounts and memoirs available in only a handful of works. Schiller's posthumously published memoir and collection of critical essays, *Living in the Number One Country: Reflections from a Critic of American Empire* (2000, hereafter *LNOC*), offers the most extensive summary of his life and critical reflections written so far. A year after Schiller's death on January 29, 2000, two minor collections of essays were published in scholarly journals. One appeared in a small section in the *Journal of Broadcast-*

ing & Electronic Media (Winter 2001, vol. 45), made up of essays by the journal editor and by Vincent Mosco and George Gerbner, two old friends. The editor wrote in his introduction that he tried "to keep the obvious affection the essay authors felt for 'Herb' from making the pieces eulogistic or laudatory." This detachment (and the objectivity it supposedly enhanced) was absent from the second and larger collection of essays that appeared in a special February 2001 issue of *Television and New Media* (vol. 2, no. 1). I was the editor of that issue and did not hesitate to invite essays that mixed fondness, affection, memoir, and intellectual analysis. Though modest in length, the issue was the only single theme work, apart from Schiller's own, devoted entirely to his life and career.

During Schiller's lifetime, two books were published in honor of his effort and influence. The most often cited of these is the 1986 collection of essays called *Communication and Domination: Essays to Honor Herbert I. Schiller*, edited by Jörg Becker, Göran Hedebro, and Leena Paldán. Apart from the introduction and the bibliography, Schiller's work was not the subject of the book, though it did represent the diverse research areas in which Schiller himself was involved. The other important work was John Lent's biographical interview with Schiller and accompanying articles on Schiller's influence in the field, published in a 1995 collection about a group of critical communication scholars called *A Different Road Taken: Profiles in Critical Communication*. Finally, Vincent Mosco has written a compact and very useful overview of Schiller's life, work, and influence in his book *The Political Economy of Communication* (1996, 82–97).

The present book is the first one devoted entirely to Schiller's work and life, but is actually no more than a complement to those mentioned here (and will join others that are being planned as I write these words). I have drawn liberally from all of these sources, in particular Schiller's own memoir and John Lent's indispensable book. The summaries of Schiller's critical thought and work are derived mainly from his books, with reference to a handful of his two hundred or so publications in English. The bibliography published here reflects nearly fifty years of output, but it is not comprehensive. It does not include titles of reprints, many occasional unpublished papers, or the myriad translations of his work. As I discovered when assembling the bibliography—a labor begun by Becker et al. and John Lent—not even Schiller kept a complete record of his achievements, nor did he know how many translations actually existed. A catalogue and archive of his own work seemed to hold little fascination for him.

The book also relies on my personal memories of Schiller and on our correspondence, in particular where I characterize his teaching and speaking styles and describe his efforts to establish a communications department at the University of California at San Diego (UCSD). In addition to our conversations and correspondence, infrequent as they were over twenty-five years, the biographical research draws on stories told to me by Schiller's friends, colleagues, and acquaintances. My Schiller story began when I was an undergraduate at UCSD in the fall of 1975. In a loose sense, I could be considered a "student of Schiller," though he never sought disciples or urged communications students to soldier forth in his name. For those of us involved in politics he was known as one of the approachable, helpful, and encouraging professors at UCSD. Herb, as many of his students called him, was "cool" when cool meant progressive, radical, or left-wing, before the word was absorbed into the commercial lexicon of MTV-style playtime. From the perspective of student activists, Schiller was, in the best sense of the word, a comrade, a companion engaged in a common experience and struggle. He was not alone in this regard, as students in this period sought out advice from the other Herbert, Herbert Marcuse, and Carlos Blanco, Will Wright, and others. Fredric Jameson, Reinhard Lettau, and Jean Franco were teaching there at the time too, and soon on a visiting basis Stanley Aronowitz, Terry Eagleton, and others passed through. You may or may not have come across these writers and intellectuals, but they formed a terrific community—not always coherently or congenially—of progressive teachers. Antiwar and antimilitarization politics already defined much of what campus life was all about at UCSD back then. These were common efforts of the time. The profs were part of the scene, but not the scene itself (a fantasy of many academics who imagine their students as unformed souls whom they mold).

As we will see, the manner in which Schiller freed up his students and their thinking about politics, media, and communication led in part to his unfreedom within the university. Not only was the communication program at UCSD reassigned under the management of more discipline-minded academics in the early 1980s, but he also spent many years at UCSD without a promotion or salary increase. Important to this story was how the communication program began as part of an alternative college within UCSD after the administration (temporarily) gave in to student demands in the late 1960s. Third College was its official name, but the students called it Lumumba-Zapata College after the Congolese and Mexican revolutionaries. It was meant to be governed from the bottom-up, and in every conceivable way the administration connived to ensure that the bottom-up arrangement would never be effective. This institutional history was important to Schiller's writing in the early 1970s.

Schiller's attitude toward the purposes of higher learning can be further explained by his biographical remarks on the way he avoided what he called "academic processing." What seemed to matter more was how his students and colleagues apprised and practiced their efforts to find the greatest insights about the social relationships that structured media, culture, communications, and information. In this regard, *my* Schiller never disconnected intellect and politics, he never detached himself from the wider world of historical events, and he never seemed to kowtow to administrators' preferences, all of which guaranteed his marginality within the university complex.

These threads of his professional life do not make sense unless they are interwoven with the personal story of Schiller's deepening political and ethical commitments and how his manner of being—his ethos of radical-humanism— came to shape his thinking, his style of writing, and his activism. After a short introduction, the book opens with a biographical essay. The background is this: born on November 5, 1919, Schiller grew up during the Great Depression in New York City where the circumstances of his childhood and youth grounded his thinking in history, his experience in class stratification, World War and its aftermath in Cold War anticommunism, neocolonialism, cultural imperialism, and anti-imperialist struggles. Subsequent chapters examine Schiller's major works chronologically in relation to changes in his life and the intellectual tasks that he saw as central to each period.

Although Herbert Schiller's life made this book possible, I don't think he would have liked it much. He wasn't the sort of person who catalogued his achievements and was uncomfortable around those who used their résumés as spotlights on themselves. He didn't keep track of the number of articles he'd written, talks he'd given, or the translations made of his books and lectures. And there were scores of them. I can only hope that I haven't garbled his ideas or made a hash of his story.

Acknowledgments

I want to thank Michael Real, Manjunath Pendakur, Janet Wasko, Jörg Becker, Graham Murdock, Cees Hamelink, Kaarle Nordenstreng, Oscar and Judy Gandy, and Patricio Tupper, who all took time to share stories about Herb Schiller, different periods of his life and the influence of his ideas. Deep gratitude goes to my favorite librarian, and all librarians everywhere who struggle to keep that "facility of democracy" open, well stocked, and free of charge. John Lent's excellent oral histories and biographical essays opened up this road for me, and Matt Cecil's insights on the McCarthyite hysteria of 1950s America helped in untold ways. Andrew Calabrese initiated this project for Rowman & Littlefield, where Brenda Hadenfeldt kept it going with a light but effective editorial touch. Ellen Seiter and Susan G. Davis gave me good advice about photographs for the book and offered to help me get them. Research funding was provided through the PSC-CUNY Research Award Program. Our union at the City University of New York, The Professional Staff Congress, gave tremendous support under the leadership of Barbara Bowen by defending our workplace from unnecessary irrationality and initiating the renewal of public higher education in New York. Most importantly, my brother Rob Maxwell helped me understand why I write. Toby Miller, my other brother, helped me understand what I write by reading drafts, suggesting improvements, and demanding more. And my wife Petra Maxwell, who pushed and pulled mightily for me to finish the book, helped me understand how I write. Our son, Luke, kept us laughing and inspired us every day to work harder to improve the society he will inherit. This book is dedicated to him.

Introduction: Reading Schiller

> I interpreted my task as trying to explain how the powerful communication system in all its spheres (film, television, publishing, the press, recording, and education) was structured, and how it created, or at least justified, inequality.
>
> —Herbert Schiller, *Living in the Number One Country* (37)

The goal of writing this book is to demonstrate how Schiller's ideas helped foster a distinct and robust discourse within critical media studies. Throughout his career, he saw his contributions to media and communication studies as historical—to explain the centrality of communication in the imperial "American Century"; to assess the rise of military-industrial enclosures around information vital for deliberative democracy; to document the social unrest and changing conditions that lead ruling groups to take greater control over sources of consciousness shaping and cultural expression; to reveal cultural-communication conditions of American imperialism; to deconstruct the hype of information and communication technologies and show instead how they were sought, developed, and appropriated by military and corporate interests; and to understand the aims and contradictions of national communication-cultural policies in order to establish a new international information order. All of these efforts "consistently aimed to situate communication studies in the wider political economic context" (Mosco 1996, 86). Schiller would have considered it a happy coincidence if these matters were of interest to communications scholars, but he thought that such agreement could only be accidental, given the prevailing disciplinary concerns, as he argued in his critique of the mainstream communications field and its "theorists of empire" (*Living in the Number One Country*, hereafter *LNOC*, 105–28).

Within the field of media studies, Schiller is best known for his research on the international political economy of communication. While there are many ways to define political economy, Vincent Mosco (1996, 25) has suggested

1

that, in general, we can think of political economy as "the study of the social relations, especially the power relations, that mutually constitute the production, distribution, and consumption of resources." Mosco divided the subfield of communication along geographical lines and identified Schiller as one of the representative figures of a "North American" approach. According to Mosco, Schiller and Dallas Smythe were "the two people who have arguably exerted the most influence on the field in this region and whose influence has been felt worldwide" (1996, 82). Smythe created the first college course in political economy of communication in the 1940s and came to focus his research on how communication facilitates the process of value creation (economic and cultural) under capitalism (for more on Smythe, see Guback 1994). In contrast, Schiller brought an interest in resource allocation to study how the distribution of information-communication resources had historically contributed to the stratification of information haves and have-nots. This particular approach to political economy focused on the class system underlying the structure of production, distribution, and consumption of media messages and communication technology, and established Schiller's reputation as a key analyst of the way ruling groups used, and abused, information and communication resources to retain their positions of power within the capitalist system. Other general features of the political economy approach outlined by Mosco—concern with the role of the state, social change, holistic analysis, moral philosophy, and political participation—are also characteristic of Schiller's work. It should be noted that "North American" political economist does not fully capture how Schiller understood his own geographical identity. His great affinity with researchers and research from Asia, Latin America, Africa, and Europe was enormously influential in his writing, perhaps more so than the work of his American compatriots. Although he wrote in an American vernacular, his work was decidedly internationalist in spirit and in the scope of issues addressed. Schiller helped established both a "robust foundation" for studying political economy of communication "in the international arena" (Mosco 1996, 94) and the internationalism that still resides at the heart of critical communication studies.

In addition to these contributions to the political economy of media processes and products, one important intellectual trait that helped make Herbert Schiller a significant figure within the field of communication was his conscious effort to address a general audience in his writing and public speeches. Schiller was highly regarded for his ability to raise clarifying questions and offer revelatory explanations in a language that just about everyone understood. This talent was key to his effectiveness as a teacher, but more importantly, it helped him become one of the most significant public intellectuals on the left to come out of the field of media and information studies. Schiller had decided early in his academic preparation that he wanted his ideas to be relevant to people's lives, not merely to the academic community. As he put it,

> Outside of the academic enterprise there is the work day, the life experiences and the day-in-day-out . . . real tribulations and trials of people. Achievement is not just to get up and make a nice little presentation that's going to be very acceptable to a half dozen or two dozen types . . . who have gone through the same process that you're being forced to go through and that is edifying to them yet eludes popular understanding. To me these are very crucial matters (quoted in Lent 1995, 137–38).

To help hone his skill as a public intellectual, Schiller worked as a radical journalist in the 1950s and continued to maintain an active interest in political journalism throughout his life, publishing numerous articles in *The Nation* and *Le Monde Diplomatique*, among other periodicals. In many ways, his journalistic practice helped shape the accessible style of writing that came to characterize his major works, and many articles were in fact expanded into chapters for his books. Such accessibility enhanced Schiller's influence among students, younger faculty, and a general, progressive readership, making him "a model of the activist scholar" (Mosco 1996, 87).

However, there is more to his public intellectual style than an accessible vocabulary and syntax. Schiller's writing and lectures were also distinguished by the implicit way he imagined his readers and audiences. While speaking to groups of people who came to learn more about the relevance of communication and information industries in their everyday lives, Schiller also gave the impression that he was addressing people as if they were, or could become, actively engaged in contemporary political life, the deliberative democratic process, and perhaps even social change. The "subject matter of my work," he said, "is not a tiny academic squabble" (quoted in Mosco 1996, 87fn.). As an activist scholar, his work focused on the media's historical significance in the long-term development of political economic arrangements in the United States and the world. As such, he cultivated a discourse that connected with the interests of the activist-citizen, broadly defined, rather than narrower interests of academics, however politically thoughtful, within communication studies. Beyond this general attitude toward his readers, we will see how his books addressed more specific audience interests in, for example, communication and foreign policy, knowledge/media work, nondominating national communication policies, or fighting the commercial takeover of culture and information.

Ironically, Schiller drew criticism from fellow academics for the results of his efforts to encourage popular understanding and engage an activist audience. Some academic critics considered Schiller's method lightweight and lacking theoretical rigor and formal discipline. Others have seen the subject matter as overly concerned with fixed structures or institutions of power and not focused enough on the creative ways that people have resisted or attempted to change the established order. While it is true that one of Schiller's arguments was that prevailing media institutions have a built-in, and self-serving, bias to see media audiences as passive subjects, he assumed he was saying this to an actively engaged reader or listener. This attitude was reinforced by a lifetime of public speaking, from the World Today lecture series at the Brooklyn Institute of Arts and Sciences, to antiwar rallies around the world, to talks "before a wide range of local, national, and international organizations" involved in media and communication policy matters (Mosco 1996, 87). Moreover, the power structure, as he understood it, was vulnerable to change caused by protest, organized political action, and internal stresses—all of which were recurring topics in his writing. And while his methods are not easily categorized according to established research practice within the field of communication and cultural analysis, he nevertheless relied on a consistent set of procedures to carry out his research and interpretations.[1] As we will see, these could be described as interpretive empirical methods that omit the formal disciplinary element of abstract theoretical exegesis, or deep interpretation of fundamental texts in communication studies and cognate fields. Although the numerous book reviews he wrote over the years indicate that he was well-versed in the field's fundamentals, it appears that he came to the conclusion that he did not need these texts to build a model or construct a theory for his research, not to mention that the technical terminology required to do so would have hindered his ability to render analysis for popular understanding. Without getting into the details of the "Schillerian" method, which is outlined in subsequent chapters, we can begin here to understand the analytics and rules of evidence he employed by a brief explanation of his approach to his first book *Mass Communications and American Empire* (hereafter *MCAE*).

Although he made no explicit statements about the formal schools of economic thought that organized this approach, his evident openness to think about the role of the nation-state and politics clearly diverged from the dominant school of neoclassical economics. He preferred to "examine the juncture where politics and economics come together," an area where contemporary economics was woefully inadequate (quoted in Lent 1995, 140). And while he never reduced his intellectual identity to any single school of thought outside the neoclassical mainstream, including Marxism, Institutionalism, Keynesianism, or neo-Mercantilism, his version of political economy resembled elements from all these traditions, in particular his attention to the historical role of the state, political power, and social conflict within economic processes. In this sense, Schiller practiced a form of radical eclecticism that allowed him to draw on diverse sources to frame his analysis and interpretation of his research.

Together with this economic orientation to the research material, his methodology in *MCAE* appears to have been influenced by his experience in the U.S. military government in postwar Germany, more of which is described in the following chapter. Schiller's characteristic use of qualitative primary sources is telling in this regard. He had learned from his proximity to the power circles in postwar Germany that "listening in" on the thinking of the main decision-makers provided strong evidence about the U.S. leadership's imperial aspirations and how this was articulated in foreign policy. The matter of choosing a particular source for *MCAE* is resolved by simple association: Schiller looked for a substantive statement or two from the people who were in a position to make a significant impact on the reality under examination—in this case, those who decided what the uses and designs for communication technology in the American-dominated imperial economy should be. In the first chapter of *MCAE*, for example, primary sources were comprised entirely by statements from President Harry Truman, presidents of the Radio Corporation of America (RCA) and Time-Life Corp, the heads of the United States Information Agency (USIA) and Radio Free Europe, a U.S. senator who was the former Deputy Secretary of State, committee reports from the 88th, 89th, and 90th Congresses on foreign policy and communications, and a couple of former government officials working in academia. This pattern was repeated throughout the book. Some of these primary sources were excerpted from the press and one from a memoir, but by and large Schiller used freely available government publications, the sort of which are today accessible at government web sites via the Internet.

This was a sourcing method that became part of Schiller's signature style and made his writing much more intelligible to the nonspecialist reader. While it is clear that Schiller did not place a high value on the specialized techniques of communication studies, or its rules of evidence, and did not employ its technical language, he was not entirely alone in using this approach for researching the domestic power structure. In the 1950s, the radical sociologist C. Wright Mills (1916–1962) had also used a similar method for understanding ruling groups in the political economy. Mills' method, as outlined for example in *The Power Elite* (1956), showed that the "higher circles" of decision-makers, while a small minority, formed a group of common interests with sufficient power to determine the political fate of the entire nation. Mills demonstrated that the increasing centralization of power among this small elite far exceeded their numbers but could be exercised through their leadership of the colossal governmental, military, and corporate bureaucracies that had grown in the postwar period. Reaching the same conclusions as Mills, Schiller discovered—both during his own wartime experience and in his subsequent research—that this power elite tended to think in a unified way, biased toward supporting each other's views on vital social matters even as they depicted their organizations as independent and democratic. The existence of such a coterie ensured that the institutions they commanded operated in a coordinated fashion. Though there is no evidence that Mills had influenced Schiller's thinking, there remain identifiable affinities between their methods (other noteworthy writers from the 1960s to the present whose methods are compatible with Schiller's include Karl Sauvant, Noam Chomsky, and Leslie Sklair, among others).[2] What Schiller's research contributed was an empirical study of the power elite's growing recognition that informational control was a key to their continued existence. With this discovery, Schiller not only offered procedures for investigating how military-industrial-corporate groups attempted to foil ordinary citizens' informational capability to scrutinize and challenge the power structure. He also invented a new critical discourse for communication studies.

A fundamental feature of this discourse was Schiller's normative assumption that media and communications technology must be used for the greater good of the world's people. However, he never pushed this ideal into hard-and-fast rules for implementing a socially productive system. That was the sort of functionalism he disdained. Instead, Schiller's arguments in *MCAE* and later work struck a balance between a universal principle in support of life-enhancing uses of communication media and deep respect for the diversity of ideas and policies generated to achieve that goal, both domestically and internationally. Still, Schiller was clear that there did exist experiences that could exemplify what to do or what not to do. As it happened, however, Schiller discovered abundant historical examples of commercial, governmental, and military bureaucracies putting communication technology to uses that undermined democratic communication processes in the developed West and yet-to-be-developed regions of the world. This discovery logically became a focus for Schiller's critique in *MCAE* of mass communication's role in the political economy.

Because of this negative emphasis, there was bound to be confusion among some readers over his approach to mass media and information technology. Most conservative commentators, and more than a few sympathetic reviewers, would accuse him of being a "technophobe" or a technology hater. The spread of Schiller's antitechnology reputation can be partly attributed to the reactionary discourse within U.S. communication studies, where there has traditionally been a strong bias against political economic research on the media and related technology. This seems especially true among technophilic communication researchers who have presumed, typically without offering proof, that Herbert Schiller's name is synonymous with thoughtless machine-smashing anarchy. In contrast, Lai-Si Tsui's close reading of Schiller's writing on technology showed that the label of technophobe represented "a caricaturing of his position" that has led to serious misreadings of Schiller's work and intent (Tsui 1995, 162).

It is more accurate to describe Schiller as a radical skeptic of technological determinism. That is, he questioned the principle, widespread in modern societies, that social or economic problems could be overcome with technological solutions alone, a subject we turn to in chapters 4 and 5. He argued further that it was precisely the pervasiveness of the myth of technology's magical powers that demonstrated the social provenance of technology: The belief was based almost entirely on self-serving representations of technology in Western economic aid policies, electronics manufacturers' advertising, technology-heavy university curricula, the U.S. space program, and other military-industrial efforts. That this institutional matrix could engender communication technology's dominant uses and define its social significance convinced Schiller that technology was in fact a social construct and not a value-neutral tool serving science and industry. As such, Schiller understood technology to have, in addition to material uses, equally important organizational, symbolic, or ideological functions for American military-industrial interests (and, in later work, for transnational capitalism generally). And yet, Schiller nevertheless treated the technological infrastructure as imminently recoverable for democratic purposes, though always with the realist's assessment of the legal and political conditions that offered protection to the well-established custodians of modern communication. In sum, Schiller's commitment to democratization, his internationalist embrace of sociopolitical diversity, and his radical skepticism about technology form the interpretive framework for his account of communications' strategic role in the expanding American empire.

Finally, while Schiller wrote from a strong conviction that historical understanding was the best way to demystify the ruling ideas of the day, he was not content to write about political economy in a style detached from the historical moment. We can only imagine how Schiller might have assessed our own historical moment and the currently fashionable discourse that says that we have entered into an unprecedented era of international dangers and opportunities for American influence around the world. Throughout his career his work remained vigilant against forgetting the evidence of military-industrial ambitions to gather power over informational resources. He also encouraged people to be alert to opportunities for social transformations that could initiate systemic change in productive, life-enhancing directions. And he argued that whatever the provenance of this political movement it would be crucial for the groups involved to take seriously informational-cultural matters. Herbert Schiller offered a compass for that radical road to change and democratic renewal. To his story we now turn.

NOTES

1. See for example, David Deacon, Michael Pickering, Peter Golding, and Graham Murdock's *Researching Communications: A Practical Guide to Methods in Media and Cultural*

Analysis (London: Arnold Publishers 1999), in which neither political economy nor Schiller appear as sources or examples—a curious absence given Golding and Murdock's work in political economy and long-term interest in Schiller's work.

2. In this context it is interesting to compare Schiller's thinking with Mills' "On Intellectual Craftsmanship," in *The Sociological Imagination* (London: Oxford University Press, 1959), 195–226.

Chapter One

Becoming a Critic of American Empire

How could I be so distant from the general thinking of the population? Was it
a personality matter, some strained sense of uniqueness? Not too much time was
spent worrying about this, but it did remain a source of wonderment.

—Herbert Schiller, *Living in the Number One Country*, 21

There is no clearer mark of historical self-understanding than to say you grew
up during the decade of the Great Depression (1929–1941). My generation
listened to our parents describe the depthless anxiety they felt as youth facing
the hunger, cold, sickness, homelessness, and other social maladies that haunted
their families and dogged them until the New Deal and World War II forced
open the job market and offered some freedom from the terror of absolute
necessity. The often dreadful memories of this period are certainly matched in
number by half-forgotten episodes and ineffable events that circumscribe a life
begun in the worst of times.

In 1929, Herbert Schiller learned about the political economy, as many ten-
year-olds first do, from exposure to the delimiting economic conditions of life
in his parent's home. Herb's father, Benjamin Schiller, was a craftsman jeweler
who lost his job after the stock market crash in 1929. He remained unem-
ployed until 1940, while Herb's mother, Gertrude, supported the family with
cleaning jobs in the New York City public school system. An uncle helped
with the rent, while Herb found odd jobs (in department stores, hotels, etc.)
that paid enough to cover transportation, meals, and occasional diversions and
pleasures. Herb attended public school, graduating from DeWitt Clinton High
School and the renowned and free City College of New York (CCNY—now
a part of the City University of New York, CUNY), where he received a
bachelor of science degree in social science and economics in 1940, six months
shy of his twenty-first birthday (*LNOC*, 11–12).

During that decade, Schiller hadn't formed a complete picture of the politi-

9

cal economy, though he had developed a generally critical attitude toward the economic system. Like most kids, his first thoughts of formal politics were "influenced entirely by what I heard my parents say," which in the case of a thirteen-year-old meant that Herbert Hoover, "the candidate of big business," would do more to help solve America's problems than Franklin Delano Roosevelt (*LNOC*, 13). But the harsh social reality of the depression would contradict his family's political outlook. Although life in the Schiller's one-bedroom apartment in the Washington Heights section of New York City allowed them to escape "destitution and dispossession," Herb came to see his father's continuing unemployment as the cause of much strife and emotional harm within his family. Daily evidence of personal depreciation offered him signs of the way the larger social system hammered the lives of individuals into deplorable states without giving them an opportunity to find relief. The economic system marginalized many people like his father without regard for their abilities, needs, pride, or sense of self-worth—the consequences of which contrasted starkly with the luster of capital and the promises of big business that had enchanted his family's political thinking.

Schiller did not fall for a hard-boiled Hollywood view of these circumstances, as exemplified by 1930s social drama films whose heroes' libertarianism, disguised as tragic heroism, was a model of resistance for the youth in this period. His life's narrative began to flow in a different direction, toward the left, as it were, of the typical American reaction to personal hardship. New York has always been a good place for an alternative education in life's twists and turns, with myriad opportunities and friendships that help expose a young man to socially progressive thinking. Most accounts of the thirties have noted, for example, the "highly politicized atmosphere" at CCNY, where Schiller earned his bachelor's degree (Mosco 1996, 85). Not surprisingly, Schiller found ways to make sense of the system without relying on the handy myths of individualism prevalent in American popular culture. Instead, he put his outrage in terms of class conflict: "From that time on, I loathed an economic system that could put a huge part of its workforce on the streets with no compunction." Schiller identified a fundamental moral source in his experience of the depression, and, from that, nourished an ethical regard for the tribulations of the laboring classes. This became the ethos, the critical manner of being, that would animate Schiller's subsequent assessments of the political economy and guide his actions: "I have never forgotten," he said, "how the deprivation of work erodes human beings, those not working and those related to them" (*LNOC*, 12).

These remarks frame Schiller's earliest ethical and political education, but do not completely explain how he managed to push his thinking as a teenager toward a budding critique of the social system. The ability to think indepen-

Herbert Schiller, Graduation Day, City College of New York, Spring 1940.

dently is, of course, available to all who receive a liberal education, especially when that education is founded in the principle that neither divine nor earthly lord shall rule over reason or individual action. The same principle impels us, shakily, to define ourselves as unique and separate from others, prodding us to live by our own wits. This road toward individuation has been known to initiate more than one personal quest to find the symbolic resources to help one survive, to teach one how to better his or her life, in short, how to "make it." Often that means acquiring an attitude of almost hyperindividualistic self-protection, captured in such clichés as "looking out for número uno," "every man for himself," and all the others that dot the mythical land of American popular culture where little swaggering heroes survive alone in a harsh world they can't change. More often this quest to find meaning and means for survival has caused individuals to make even more deeply significant modifications to the liberal education's secular ideals by choosing to pattern one's life according to formal religious beliefs and practices. Paradoxically, when this happens, American individualism ends up forfeiting a predicate of its freedom, adopting instead a communal belief that a divine presence has structured the world into a vertical order of power relationships in which each person's fate and fortune is predetermined for the good of the whole.

Growing up, Schiller experienced neither the psychic rewards of individualism nor religious solace, a peculiar absence of cultural influence that he came to believe liberated his thinking about the social conditions of life around him. As he explains, his mother and father were not actively atheistic, just too caught up in the shared aims of "getting food on the table and securing for their son the best education they could not actually afford." At the end of his life, Schiller continued to feel "fortunate to have escaped from the confines of orthodoxy and parochialism" that surrounded those steeped in religious belief (*LNOC*, 13).

If religion did not play a role in shaping Schiller's temperament and manner of being, humor and the progressive cultural environment of 1930s New York certainly did. By all accounts, Schiller was always funny. He was a witty conversationalist and, like many New Yorkers, could find an amusing side to any story, no matter how dreadful the surrounding events. We might imagine him in this way, as a young man engaged in fast-talking banter with a group of nimble-tongued New Yorkers dissecting the world's troubles, a twinkle in his eye as he searched for the right punch line to bring out a bit of life's comic twists and turns. We might imagine the cultural experiences of his youth in a time and place in which the establishment had loosened control over social and artistic expression. After all, public funding of cultural works in 1930s exposed New Yorkers, and many other Americans, to a particularly vibrant period of socially concerned expression. As Schiller recalled, "Plays were financially underwritten with public funds, staged excitingly, and captured new audiences. Novels with social themes poured forth. Murals were painted in public buildings. Guidebooks were produced that detailed the many sites and voices of a noncorporate America. . . . Social concerns infused content. The works produced were meaningful to those who encountered them" (*Culture Inc.* 1989, 159). It was just such a milieu wherein a young man free of the influences of political and religious orthodoxy could have nurtured his acuity and wit to become, as Schiller did, a raconteur who enjoyed more than anything sharing a good story and a laugh at the expense of the powerful.

This secular, nonindividualistic, and ironic orientation to life in a city of robust debate and critical-cultural ferment may have helped Schiller transform the "sadness and resentment" instilled in him by socioeconomic misfortune into a critical, and, as it happened, abiding antagonism toward a class system that he felt had caused "ten years of human wastage" (*LNOC*, 13). If the socially organized political economy (as opposed to some divine, central presence) caused a decade of suffering, then clearly human intervention could create fundamentally different conditions. The political economy was mutable. It could have organized work and workers differently to ensure such suffering never happened, but it didn't. So a teenager began to think that an economic system could be called to account for its deplorable deeds. The absence of religiosity helped free Schiller's thought to develop his leftward angle for understanding his family's plight. It also may have prepared him to feel that entreaties for submission to a putatively benevolent big business resonated far too much with the false hope offered by religious authorities, and so deserved all the mockery that he could muster.

Schiller's ideas of justice were becoming clearer in this context. He did not believe in a theistic mission to help the poor. Nor did he believe in an abstract idea of rights and privileges. He did not speak of his father's right to employment, what in contemporary conservative vocabulary is called a "right to work." There is no mention in his memoirs that any individual entitlements had been denied, the lack of which was felt as the disturbance of the safe confines of his small family circle. Instead, right and wrong had more to do with how the "have-nots" fared, how the weakest survived, and how this was everyone's concern. To depict conditions any other way would be ludicrous. Thus Schiller's growing political sensibility began to take shape as a secular ethics centered on social responsibilities, needs, relationships, and on the interdependence of the members of that society rather than as an espousal of religious duty or of the individual's rights and preserve. This ethico-political orientation would eventually be anchored in Schiller's pronounced analytical questions about who controlled this economic system and how power relationships came to be structured.

Empires come with spectacular means to beguile their subjects, and Schiller began to see how "mind management," as he would later call it, affected the ability of his own family to discern the ways that big business contributed to their misfortunes. Empires also decline, some in even more stunning fashion than their rise to domination, but they never go without a fight. Schiller's resistance to an empire's seductions was galvanized at a moment in history when the United States established its global hegemony and developed the most sophisticated means of controlling public perceptions of the international political economy. This was illustrated in his personal reflections on his life after he graduated from college, when the war economy finally brought his family relief and him a civilian job in the U.S. War Department before and after military service. Three key encounters with the wider political economy solidified his budding political convictions and sense of justice: American racism, European colonialism in North Africa, and the tragic costs of war and postwar class conflict.

In the fall of 1941, Schiller moved to Washington, D.C., where he worked for the Department of Labor. A few months later, after the United States entered the war, Schiller began work at the War Production Board (WPB). His degrees in economics, including a master's degree in economics from Columbia University received in 1941, gave him the credentials for a job as a junior industrial economist in the WPB's bureau of research and statistics. Already predisposed to see the economy as a malleable system, Schiller now worked in the lower levels of the agency charged with the singular tasks of directing all war-related production during World War II. This included the allocation and distribution of scarce resources for the purpose of transforming the peacetime economy into a war economy, while at the same time prohibiting industrial activities the WPB deemed dispensable. Schiller was working at the center of economic power in which essential aspects of the nation's economy were controlled by "dollar-a-year" antiunion industrial business executives. Inured to the seductive power of the big money boys, Schiller joined the United Federal Workers union and began recruiting others, mostly unsuccessfully (the WPB was superceded by the Civilian Production Administration in the fall of 1945 to reconvert the economy).

Also in Washington, Schiller became more conscious of the real force of Jim Crow laws that barred African Americans from access to jobs and public places such as restaurants, hotels, and other facilities. Although "New York at the time [was] scarcely less segregated," he had not yet witnessed the same level of explicit, face-to-face, and institutional racism as he would upon entering Virginia from the District of Columbia where for the first time he saw signs that instructed "Negroes" to refrain from entering public parks, to eat in separate dining areas, and to wait in separate food lines. He knew that "New York apartheid was very real," but he first came to understand how it could be enforced "as a legally coercive system" while living in the Washington area. "To a twenty-one-year-old raised in New York City," he wrote, "Washington's overt racism was a shock" (*LNOC*, 15). Here he was again faced with another glaring contradiction that demanded a critical awakening: The "dynamic center of the war effort to defeat the Nazis and the fascists was itself a profoundly antidemocratic place" (*LNOC*, 14). Nevertheless, Washington proved to be a "stark prelude" to what Schiller would confront after his induction into the military in 1942.

Schiller spent the bulk of military service in North Africa after 1943, mostly in Morocco, where very quickly he learned that his knowledge of the desperate conditions of "Depression-stricken America" was insufficient to prepare him for the sight of the tragic dereliction that colonialism brought to the people of

Africa. In Casablanca he was shaken by the existence of the *"bidonvilles*, tin can settlements, made up of discarded oil drums and cardboard cartons" that "surrounded the city, homes to thousands of people" (*LNOC*, 17). He understood that bloody colonialism caused this dispossession, again narrowing his focus to the social and economic system and its leaders who shamelessly discarded an entire people. In this case, the French "were still the reigning colonial power across the rim of North Africa," though "it was clear, even in 1943, their rule was coming to a close" (*LNOC*, 17). Taking their place was the United States' massive military presence, accompanied by well-stocked commissaries, black-marketed American goods, and Hollywood movies. Schiller saw the United States as a swaggering "new power, with its material riches and dazzling images . . . nonchalantly elbowing out the once dominating authority" (*LNOC*, 18).

The young man who came to loath an economic system that could abandon its own people without compunction now considered the wider dimension of cruelty of the class system as it spread via the international political economy. Schiller's interpretation of the class divisions in the United States began to broaden into his thinking of a model of domination that operated on a global scale. North Africa brought about this ethical and political awakening. "For me," Schiller wrote,

> the North African interlude was a powerful prod to consciousness. What later came to be called, always euphemistically and often deceitfully, the Third World, the developing world, and, most recently, "emerging markets," continues to be, as I then began to understand it, the part of the world where great numbers of people live and die under frightfully deprived conditions. In their midst are enclaves of lavish wealth and power. Over time, I realized that these tragic destinies continue to be ordered by foreign owners and investors, and local oligarchs, whose one public concern is undisturbed profit making. This was the burden that the "advanced" West, and the United States in particular, imposed, and continues to impose, on the poorest and weakest peoples worldwide for half a century. (*LNOC*, 18)

As Schiller's political understanding and analysis of the political economy formed, his interest in the world around him and his powers of observation sharpened. He was curious about how societies were organized, what people did to survive, how the political powers interact with economic interests. Yet he does not credit his questioning or insight to his college education, which he called "shallow and superficial" in areas of instruction about "the driving forces" and "basic relationships that comprise the prevailing system of production and consumption" (*LNOC*, 19).

In November 1945, at the age of twenty-six, Herbert Schiller was honorably discharged from the army as a corporal. He was a handsome, brown-eyed man, weighing a spare 144 pounds at six feet, one inch tall, with dark, wavy hair beginning to show hints of silver. He served two years, three months, and four days, almost entirely in North Africa, as an "information and education specialist clerk typist" without participating in any combat. After returning to the United States, his furlough from his appointment at the War Production Board (by then, the Civilian Production Administration) continued until March 1946. Schiller remembered the three months he spent in New York between late November and early March as a hopeless effort to "jump into the postwar boom that was swirling about." Instead, he found a new civilian job within the War Department and requested a transfer. On March 8, his position as assistant economist was officially terminated, and two days later he became a War Department labor economist in the European Theater's Office of Military Government for Germany, Manpower Division at Berlin. This job was part of the U.S. government's massive investment to restructure the German economy and, presumably, kick start democratization. Schiller lived in Germany until the summer of 1948, when his employment contract expired.

With the optimism of a twenty-six-year-old, Schiller traveled to Germany believing he was about to join an effort with potential to create "a new Germany in a truly democratic way," abolishing all the old institutional structures that made feasible the "fascist movement and government [and] political extremes that had developed in the fascist period" (quoted in Lent 1995, 136). Again, Schiller became immersed in a dynamic learning situation outside a university environment that would deepen his critical ethos and political sensibility. This real-life education combined with his youthful sense of adventure and sheer luck to be in a position to witness the relationships that formed the power structure around him.

Still, his life in Germany was not all work related. Schiller had also fallen in love with the beautiful twenty-year-old Anita Rosenbaum, whom he had met in New York City. During a week in early November 1946, Rosenbaum traveled from New York to France, where she joined Schiller, who had been granted ten days leave of duty. While there, on Schiller's twenty-seventh birthday, the couple were married in a civil ceremony conducted by the mayor of the Seventh Arrondissement of Paris. They returned to Berlin together and, over the next two years, took advantage of several brief leaves of duty to tour Czechoslovakia, Yugoslavia, France, and Germany.

Along with these exciting personal changes, Schiller's responsibilities in the military government, in contrast to those at the WPB, were about to initiate him into a new phase of political understanding of the global power structure. His job, though at a very junior level, brought him "close to important decisionmaking," where he found himself present at "high level meetings, close to high level relationships," and to "people in important positions" (quoted in

Lent 1995, 136). He was able to learn firsthand how the controllers of a society "behaved, who they were, and what kind of outlooks they had, and, more than any of this, to see the policies themselves" (quoted in Lent, 136). Schiller was "as close as you can get in the social science area to a laboratory experiment" in practical political science and economic engineering. He directly observed the effects of "the deliberate reconstruction of [a] political economy," which a devastating war had turned into a "socioeconomic political vacuum" (quoted in Lent, 136–37). He watched as the U.S. Military Government filled the vacuum in a very short time with "the preferred kinds of institutional arrangements that would lead to certain types of outcomes—outcomes in terms of economic activity, in terms of political structure, in terms of social consciousness" (quoted in Lent, 137).

The U.S. Military Government in Germany was charged with implementing a policy to restabilize the political and economic order in postwar Germany, but took as its focus Germany's future role in the larger international political economy, which the United States sought to control. Between 1946 and 1948, a break in relations between the United States and Soviet Union occurred over the direction and implementation of reforms, in particular the use of reparations. This happened simultaneously with a shift from the harsh deindustrialization reforms set out in the 1944 Morgenthau Plan (named for then U.S. Treasury Secretary Henry Morgenthau) to those of the Marshall Plan (first articulated in 1947 by then U.S. Secretary of State George C. Marshall). The United States primarily saw reparations as an instrument of American security and dominance in the political economy of the region, partly via economic disarmament of Germany (reducing war potential) and partly by paying for the German economy to play a central role in European economic recovery (rebuilding the industrial and financial base).

In 1946, around the time Schiller arrived in Berlin, the U.S. Military Government ordered a halt to reparations payments out of the Western zones to the Soviets (Kindleberger 1973, np). The Americans refused to yield to Soviet demands for badly needed resources from German reparations, affirming for the Soviets the greediness of U.S. capitalistic self-interest. Because Moscow resisted seeing Germany as a single economic unit, as set out by the U.S. State Department in *U.S. Economic Policy toward Germany* (written by Walt Rostow in 1946), it wouldn't cooperate by revealing information related to such things as the quantity of machinery, goods, and labor it had claimed in the Russian zone of Germany (Kindleberger 1973, np).

To U.S. decision-makers, the Soviet Union's plans for reparations appeared to threaten the goals of the United States, especially demands that directed wealth from renewed German production toward the damaged Russian society (which had lost twenty million lives in the fight against Nazi Germany). As noted by Charles P. Kindleberger, chief of the German and Austrian Economic Affairs Division of the Department of State between 1945 and 1948, "The Russians gave us a terrible time on these issues." But, added Kindleberger, "It's hard to say in retrospect, and even at the time it was hard to say they were terribly wrong" (Kindleberger 1973, np). Nevertheless, Washington reacted by cutting off the Soviets to reparations and then implementing the Marshall Plan aid program in Western Europe, which made economic aid contingent on the exclusion of Communists from government (*LNOC*, 24). This two-pronged strategy of U.S. foreign policy hobbled Soviet reconstruction and helped secure, against the growing appeal of socialism in Western Europe, European national leaders' endorsement of the Americanization of the international market system.

So the creation of Germany "as a firm ally against the East" required the creation of a political economy shorn of socialistic potential, and that meant risking reestablishing the very "same market monopoly society" in Germany that had provided the conditions for the dismantlement of Germany's democratic institutions in the 1930s (quoted in Lent 1995, 136, 138). Schiller learned from this "hard-to-come-by instruction how a terribly battered, industrialized market economy is rehabilitated by a self-interested class ally" (*LNOC*, 19). His optimism faded as "all of the old institutional structures prevailed," and were eventually organized into a system that he had already seen cause much misery (Lent 1995, 136). He thus became "disgusted with official U.S. policy in Germany," especially with its core "anti-communism," which seemed to him to degrade the quality of decision-making and create the potential for recapitulating antidemocratic horrors that prevailed under the Nazis. He saw demagogic anticommunism on the one hand generating a "terribly wrong and falsified assessment of Russian aims" and, on the other, dismantling, with covert military pressure and bloody espionage, the democratic movements and major political parties in Western Europe, which were "led by Communists and socialists . . . as a result of their anti-fascist leadership during the war" (*LNOC*, 19, 24).

Anticommunism had been a predicate of U.S. foreign policy since the Russian Revolution, but became the defining ideology of U.S. foreign policy after World War II. The U.S. leadership's postwar reaction reinforced the militarized efforts to crush support for experiments in progressive economic models everywhere, in particular socially planned approaches, and helped anticommunism grow into "a full-blown national environment" back in the United States (*LNOC*, 19). When Schiller returned to the United States in 1948, this policy had been translated into a domestic war against civilians to intimidate free thought, silence speech, or dismantle any institutional arrangements that diverged from free-market, monopoly capitalism. Schiller became more interested in formal politics at this time, seeking out alternatives in the Progressive Party of Henry Wallace, former vice president under Roosevelt, who offered a reasonably informed position on Soviet foreign policy (*LNOC*, 20). When the Progressives faded in the aftermath of Truman's narrow election, Schiller's interest in party politics shifted toward more radical independent political work and the micropolitics of everyday survival. This was no small matter for any thirty-year-old man who had to find work to contribute his share to supporting a household, which would soon include two baby boys. But then survival also meant finding breathing space in the poisonous atmosphere "of what came to be known as McCarthyism," which was "saturated with fear and hatred . . . overhung by the reality of investigating commissions, firings, the blacklist, and the generalized repression and coercion" (*LNOC*, 20–21).

Here Schiller was referring to well-publicized actions of the House Un-American Activities Committee (HUAC). In 1938, a year after its creation, the HUAC turned away from investigating and exposing domestic fascism in the U.S. to become an extrajudicial, anticommunist court of inquisition, thanks largely to the efforts of committee members, including its founder, who were Ku Klux Klan cronies (the Klan was halfheartedly proposed as HUAC's first target). In the 1940s, HUAC had scandalized and slandered the names of bookstores, college professors, civil rights activists, and writers with alleged communist affiliation (including an attempt to label as un-American the founding father of critical political economy of communications, Dallas Smythe; see Lent 1995, 28). They even persecuted Americans who fought to defend democracy in Europe before the United States entered the war, including those who joined the Lincoln Brigades to fight fascism in Spain during the Spanish Civil War (1936–1939), and those who spoke out against Hitler and Mussolini in the 1930s (these people were later dubbed "premature antifascists"). By war's end and throughout the 1950s, HUAC investigations destroyed the lives and livelihoods of many progressives in an effort to erase their contributions to American society and bar them from positions of influence. By the time Senator Joseph McCarthy came to lead the HUAC attack between 1951 and 1954, and give this dark decade a name, many prominent figures in government, journalism, film, radio and TV, and higher education had been subpoenaed, publicly excoriated, ordered to "name the names" of suspicious characters, communists, or anyone holding opinions that dissented from government doctrine and the capitalist system.

While the covert investigations of the Federal Bureau of Investigation (FBI) may have had less publicity than HUAC—indeed, the FBI often manipulated press reports to keep its methods secret (Cecil 2002)—their effects were known by anyone in the late 1940s and early 1950s who was mildly aware of diminishing civil liberties or held opinions opposed to U.S. foreign policy. Schiller remembered how it seemed over the next few years—that progressive, alternative views were becoming "less and less visible, eventually approaching underground status" as a result of this "ferocious state-directed intimidation" (*LNOC*, 22–23). Later in the decade, domestic spying in the United States expanded in this period as the FBI began an intense anticommunist operation designed to exploit the internal conflicts within the American Communist Party and socialist movement that had erupted in 1956 after the Soviet leader, Nikita Khrushchev, denounced Stalin and Stalin-era horrors in the Soviet Union. There were already a number of FBI investigations under way, but a new order of urgency was initiated in that year with the covert operations known as the "Counter-Intelligence Programs," or COINTELPRO. Also throughout the 1950s into the 1970s, the FBI compiled what it called "the Security Index" (SI), which was the list of people the FBI would seize as national security threats should the United States come under attack (reportedly, the SI list at one time contained the names of a half million "suspects"). Many socially progressive people were harmed in this period by these attacks on civil liberties—from Martin Luther King and free speech activists in the antiwar and student movements to the radical Black Panthers movement in the 1960s.[1]

In the late 1940s, Schiller considered staying in Europe to obtain a doctorate and perhaps work as a writer and journalist, but he and his wife decided instead to return to the Bronx, New York, in the summer of 1948, at which time his contract with the War Department was officially complete. Entitled to four years of college under the G.I. Bill of Rights, Schiller entered Columbia University in September of 1948 to get a Ph.D. in history, and began to look for teaching jobs and fellowships. By 1949, he had picked up a part-time teaching job as an evening lecturer in economics at the Bernard Baruch business school of the City College of New York (now Baruch College-CUNY). In 1950, he began his first full-time job as an instructor of economics at the Pratt Institute in Brooklyn, where he would be promoted to assistant professor in 1953. By 1950 it was clear that Schiller would be unable to finish his doctorate at Columbia, for lack of evening courses and his full-time work, so he transferred to New York University (NYU), where he began a decade-long push to finish his Ph.D. in economics. By the early 1950s, Herbert and Anita Schiller lived in Brooklyn with their two sons, Dan and Zach. Schiller was taking classes at NYU at least one evening each week and teaching over twenty hours a week at Pratt and CCNY, making very little money. His doctoral education was almost haphazard as a result. "Nobody knew who I was," he said of his professors. His "only expectation was just to stay enrolled to be able to maintain [his] matriculation. If anything ever came out of it," he said, "it would be a miracle" (quoted in Lent 1995, 137).

This vibrant teacher, student, and father was also tirelessly committed to becoming more actively involved politically—that is, without attracting too much "attention of the new vigilantism" (*LNOC*, 22). So, in this "era of semi-hysteria," he began to put his critical analysis in publishable form. By 1950, he had become "a part-time, unpaid, radical journalist," delivering short articles on U.S. foreign policy to the Labor Research Association (LRA), a "tiny research group that critically scrutinized the corporate features of the American economy" (*LNOC*, 22). These weekly and biweekly pieces were published pseudonymously with the LRA byline. At first, Schiller "felt more than a little anxiety" about using his own name because his articles challenged the conventional portrayal and misconceptions of U.S. policy in the mainstream press. The cultural environment was contaminated to such a degree by state-sponsored attacks on free speech and political association that Schiller justifiably believed that his "extracurricular activity" could become part of an investigation that might threaten his income and family. He recognized that, "Pitiful as these jobs were monetarily, they would have disappeared immediately" had a HUAC or FBI investigation created a scandal for his employers. He remembered that, "Each visit to the LRA office on East Eighteenth Street in New York City . . . seemed fraught." After all, "Paranoia prevailed in the country at large, and I was entitled to exhibit mine by walking rapidly, or averting my face, and worrying incessantly that I was being photographed entering the building or the office" (*LNOC*, 23). But Schiller was undaunted and his radical writing efforts "continued for several years, though [his] productivity, and . . . paranoia tailed off after the mid 1950s" (*LNOC*, 23).

Although Schiller said he adopted a low profile as a writer for the LRA, his achievements in fact demonstrate how he actually grew more outspoken during McCarthyite hysteria. This gloomy period in American life could not dampen Schiller's high level of energy and sense of humor. He must have welcomed the demise of Joe McCarthy in the mid 1950s, and certainly would have been relieved by the slight, though temporary, waning in Cold War military buildup at that time. In 1955 and 1956, he started to publish under his own name, producing two scholarly pieces that revisited themes from his LRA work: one on the Cold War's political function of extending American economic power internationally, and one showing that American economic policy, and not the Soviet Union's, was the actual source of anti-Americanism within the indigenous radical movements in Western Europe (*LNOC*, 23). These efforts showed his resistance to the suffocating intimidation that had affected many others during the 1950s. From the time he wrote "The World Bank: Agency for Wall Street's Cold War" in 1950 for the LRA to the day of publishing *Mass Communications and American Empire* in 1969, Schiller's writing, speaking, and teaching became more openly critical of U.S. policy, showing the destructive power of United States-controlled economic aid instruments such as the World Bank and International Monetary Fund (IMF). In 1950 he wrote accounts about how economic assistance was systematically "withheld from poor, socialist, or socialist-inclined states in the post-war years" (*LNOC*, 30). Fifty years later he was still challenging these policies as the IMF and World Bank continued to keep postcolonial countries from emerging from abject conditions of poverty. "For half a century," Schiller wrote, "these institutions, with dependence on the United States structured into their voting arrangements, have decided the policies that countries seeking aid and loans would have to follow" (*LNOC*, 190).

Apart from his writing, perhaps the greatest breathing space for Schiller to work and think was in the academic establishment, where he increasingly earned a reasonable livelihood as a teacher. Schiller loved to teach, and the classroom was an energizing place for him, where he developed a teaching style that combined his ethical sensibilities, his already highly advanced skills as an incisive observer of the political economy, and a remarkable ability to find humorous content in anything he was talking about. Apart from making a positive contribution by helping his students comprehend the social world, Schiller enjoyed a talent to lecture with terrific wit and irony. As one observer noted years later, while his lectures were invariably critical of American policy and popular culture, the "entertainment value was always high" (Webster 2001, 31). His teaching was highly regarded, though such appreciation, where it occurred, did not mean that Schiller felt entirely at home in the conservative culture of the academy.

Becoming a critical thinker inside the American academic enterprise depends on one's ability to escape the strictures of that enterprise, especially when trying to define the utility of your work for yourself. By the time he received his Ph.D. in 1960, his university education could not erase the lessons Schiller gained during the years of depression, war, and postwar "reconstruction." He was forty years old and finally had "*the credential*" to move ahead in the academic world, but he almost completely lacked a sense of identification with that world. "I never became part of that systematized structure of being led, being told, being influenced, being forced all the way along the line," he said, "even if one is not totally conscious of being put into a mold." He learned that this was not a deficiency but, rather like his appreciation of having no religious training, "something that, though very intangible, was very important." He had

escaped this process of education, which, for the most part, may be far more successful in structuring the very nature of how people view processes and view the social order and their expectations. . . . And also, of course—and this may be the most important of all—one doesn't have the view that the academic enterprise is the "be-all" and "end-all" of life. (quoted in Lent 1995, 137–38)

For Schiller, teachers, researchers, and academic professionals were all living inside the contemporary political economy, however hard they tried to shelter themselves in an isolated zone of academic disputes alone. What he had to say about the work of other intellectuals went to understanding whether they offered insight about the political and economic processes that structured the system of economic power and political control. He may have appreciated the narrow professional concerns of academic research, but Schiller did not approach these matters as the "be-all" and "end-all" of his thought. By refusing to fully embrace the academic enterprise, he was never seduced into ivory tower detachment, which would have taken him outside of the historical flow of events around him. Thus his thought, his many intellectual interests, and his hard work were all anchored in a dynamic way to world history and only casually to the academic world.

Tenure and promotion to associate professor could not change this course of intellectual development, which led to the prolific publication of over forty articles and a book during the 1960s. It also led to a certain professional stature that allowed Schiller to become, as he said with a bit of ironic detachment, "a more respectable member of the academic community" (quoted in Lent 1995, 139). As such, his possibilities for advancement and a higher income multiplied significantly after he received his Ph.D. In 1961, Schiller took leave from the Pratt Institute for a one-year visiting professorship at the University of Illinois in Urbana, returning to Pratt the following year with a promotion to full professor and the position as chairman of the social studies department. Schiller's superiors at Pratt wanted very much to keep him on staff, but the salary was comparatively low on the national scale. His colleagues were thus sorely disappointed to have lost him the following year when, in 1963, Schiller accepted a job as associate research professor in the Bureau of Economics and Business Research at the University of Illinois (Lent 1995, 132).

Until 1965, Schiller's published scholarly work took up general questions of resource distribution and economic development, focusing on particular issues of location analysis within economic geography. Schiller sought to open up economic study to account for political decision-making affecting development, without losing sight of the effects on the ground of political and economic interactions. When he turned to the study of communication structures and processes in the mid 1960s, Schiller transposed resource distribution, location analysis, and historical and economic geography onto his new subject of inquiry. He also maintained an active interest in political journalism, which he then took up with an occasional article on international communication policy, starting with a 1965 article in *The Nation* entitled "The Sovereign State of Comsat." One of his first conference papers to deal with information within a framework of economic development research was on the radio spectrum as a natural resource. "That was not an original idea," Schiller would recall, because "the radio spectrum is [already] regarded as a natural resource . . . but I tried to look at it as [it] was being used or abused, and what were the institutional factors that led to the character of the utilization" (quoted in Lent 1995, 140–41). Schiller drew on twenty years of experience, going back to his days as an economic analyst in the 1940s, to rethink the economic organization and development problems in his political analysis of the radio spectrum (something Dallas Smythe had also worked on). Henceforth, Schiller focused all of his energy on the communication and information question.

His approach was new in U.S. international communication research, though he turned to communication following the trail opened up by Dallas Smythe, who had been teaching courses on the political economy of communication since 1948, starting at the University of Illinois. After Smythe left Illinois in 1963, the course eventually found its way to Schiller, who benefited from the new material and the impetus it gave him for an original line of intellectual inquiry. Also at the Bureau of Economics and Business Research, where he was promoted to full professor in 1966, Schiller was blessed to work under an open-minded director who did not question this newfound interest in communication. Everything that had concerned Schiller over the past twenty years of intellectual work converged in the communications research area: U.S. foreign policy and militarism, technology and working conditions, social effects of monopoly market systems, the state's role in overcoming crises, alternative economic systems, developments in poor regions of the world, and so on. If Schiller's work was energized by his discovery that communication was at the heart of these processes, the explosion of writing that followed was certainly amplified by the world historical events of the 1960s.

Around the world, during the 1950s and 1960s, anticolonial movements and liberated excolonies began to challenge international political reality with demands for change, not only in the global economic system but, as Schiller observed, in the informational structures that inhere in that system as well. Schiller "became engaged in the short-lived efforts of the ex-colonial world to restructure the global economy into a more equitable and life-enhancing living space." He followed with great interest and hope the "numbers of poor nations, some still led by their liberation heroes—Nehru in India, Sukarno in Indonesia, Tito in Yugoslavia, Castro in Cuba, Nasser in Egypt, Ben Bella in Algeria, Nkrumah in Ghana, and others in Kenya, Angola, Mozambique, and elsewhere"—as they sought to restructure the global distribution of material and informational resources (*LNOC*, 33–34).

These disruptions within the postwar world order provided political sustenance to Schiller's enormous intellectual output in the mid to late 1960s. At the same time, he was encouraged by the growing resistance to the inherited conservatism of 1950s America. The free speech movement was mounting as student protests against the U.S. war in Vietnam became more numerous and hard for media and government to discredit. The civil rights movement gained momentum against pervasive white supremacy in the law and popular culture, and the women's liberation movement of the 1960s challenged the orthodoxy and institutionalization of unequal relations between the sexes. Encouraging signs of this rebellion were available in the 1950s, but the "barbarous colonial war" in Vietnam seemed to shake the country to consciousness (*LNOC*, 32). This was also the height of the American postwar economic boom, and a time when the universities were bursting at the seams, not only with first-generation college students, but with enormous resources to support programs that didn't merely serve the dominant interests. Schiller found "a certain amount of space" then that he would not experience again, for "things were more fluid or open, if only temporarily" (quoted in Lent 1995, 141).

Also throughout the 1960s, Schiller was a regular speaker in the World Today lecture series at the Brooklyn Institute of Arts and Sciences. His public speaking engagements multiplied, though not yet in the area of communication. His virtuoso speeches on U.S. foreign policy and military-corporate imperatives made him a very popular pick for antiwar rallies, political gatherings, and so on. He was especially pleased by these invitations and would travel anywhere in the world to speak. At the height of the antiwar movement (the moratorium, as it was known then), while Schiller was traveling on a speaking tour in Australia, he received an invitation to address the waterside workers of Sydney on the subject of Vietnam and U.S. foreign policy. At that meeting he learned that Paul Robeson, the great African American activist and performer, stood in the same spot years earlier, inspiring the "wharfies" with speech, song, and protest. The memory always seemed to fill him with that special delight of living in the big picture of historical processes and the world struggle for progressive change. He was also very engaged throughout the 1960s at home in more local matters. He was not only committed to student and faculty coalition-building and activism to stop the war and war-related research in the university, but he became involved in the American Association of University Professors, serving as chapter president at Pratt, secretary of the Illinois chapter, and then vice president of the Illinois chapter (Lent 1995, 132).

This is how Schiller remembers some of the radicalism that breached the dominant perceptions of American empire in the 1960s:

The anti-war movement grew stronger as the war continued, but the propaganda for the war was no less intense, as the specter of one anticommunist domino after another falling to the Reds became an unrelieved Washington refrain. And the media were fully complicit in supporting the war in the early years of the conflict. What turned the tide was the strength of the Vietnamese resistance, as the costs of waging the war reduced the national budget to a shambles. The decisive cost at home, however, was in the lost blood and lives of American youth. When domestic anger and shock reached a level dangerous to social stability, parts of the establishment and the media broke the prowar consensus and the unraveling was underway. Even in such a relatively remote place as central Illinois, long the site of a "jock" university with row upon row of fraternity and sorority houses, the war jolted the campus out of its play routines. (*LNOC*, 32)

Another important condition for Schiller's burst of intellectual activity, though less interesting than the worldwide political movements that inspired him, was the creative freedom he credited to his ongoing academic anonymity, though now in the politically conservative field of mass communication. He was a newcomer to the relatively new field of communications in the 1960s, an outsider among a small but established group of communication scholars. Daniel Lerner, for instance, was a leader in the field of international communications and treated Schiller's anti-imperialist perspective as naïve and Schiller as a nobody. Lerner once shared Schiller's critical view of the world during the days of antifascist struggle. But in the postwar period, Lerner, along with Wilbur Schramm, Ithiel de Sola Pool, and other communication experts, became a gung ho cold warrior, recasting psychological warfare research in the American academy as mass communication research, a more neutral sounding enterprise. This helped ensure that American international communication research would be more congenial with the objectives and aims of U.S. foreign policy. Schramm, often credited as the founder of contemporary mass communication studies, was an FBI informer, CIA contract man, and remained throughout his career, along with Lerner and Pool, close to military and intelligence communities, promoting a supremacist view of Western culture and technology via the reputedly objective norms of social science methodology (see Simpson 1994). Schramm and Lerner's efforts in the anticommunist, pro–Western crusade earned them top spots in the academy as leaders in the field of international communication research (Lent 1995, 32, 138). To them, there was no reason to pay attention to what this Johnny-come-lately was saying or writing. "That would be conferring legitimacy on the upstart," as Schiller put it. Being considered a "nobody" in the academic field of international communications kept the spotlight off of Schiller just long enough for him to gather sufficient research on the global communication system and eventually produce "a body of material that finally could not be ignored" (quoted in Lent 1995, 141).

Up to this point, Schiller's exposure in American academia relied on the appeal of his radical approach among younger faculty and graduate students looking for sources to challenge the conventional thinking of established figures such as Lerner and Schramm. When his book *Mass Communications and American Empire* appeared in 1969, it had little impact on the closed-minded discipline in the United States. Indeed, it was overlooked by the major academic journals and mainstream book review circles, except for Robert Shayon, the TV editor at the *Saturday Review.* Shayon's review praised the book as the first to challenge the cold war assumptions in communications, bringing Schiller's work to the attention of other writers, in particular progressive and independent journalists and publishers. Inside the United States, Schiller thus found a small, committed, and growing readership. In a very short time, however, Schiller's oppositional approach to standard American communications scholarship received a hardier welcome from a larger and more open-minded audience of intellectuals and activists outside the United States. The following chapter will show why.

This episode brings the story to a point in which a more detailed examination of Schiller's writing is warranted. The aim thus far has been to sketch out the contours of Herbert Schiller's intellectual biography, beginning at the place and time of his youth in New York City to his days in Washington and North Africa during World War II and Germany in the postwar period, to his stint as a radical journalist, and then as a struggling academic during the frozen days of McCarthyism and the fluid days of the 1960s. His early exposure to what he saw as the fundamental flaws in the capitalist political economy sparked a political awareness and radical ethos that informed his judgments and interpretation of the political economy, and helped set in motion a series of choices, mixed with luck and the accidents of being in the right place at the right time, to shape the course of his life's story.

If this brief account of Schiller's life resonates with contemporary experience, it is because it offers recognizable moments of enthusiasm, despair, suspicions, a sense of duty, resolve, anger, ironic detachment, conscientiousness, and commitment. These are components of a certain manner, temperament, and style—taken together to form a structure of feeling, as the British writer Raymond Williams might have said—that can inspire us in some way as teachers, public intellectuals, students, or activists. Many continuities linking our own and Schiller's time will be discussed in subsequent chapters. If Schiller could suggest what should be done as we consider our place in this flow of history, it is this: First, remember that the system is mutable, and we are entitled to be outraged "over a course of events that could have had different outcomes."

Then never "imagine accommodation or passivity in the face of what some-times seem[s] lunatic, at other times calculated, aggressions against ordinary people's lives and well-being" (*LNOC*, 45). Alas, "American policy and actions have for half a century repeatedly frustrated initiatives for a better and more diverse world. It is an awesome indictment" (*LNOC*, 46). That's a good way to think of the work that follows.

NOTE

1. Laws enacted in the 1970s to rein in covert surveillance operations and prevent such violations of rights and civil liberties as those that occurred during COINTELPRO were turned back by the 2001 USA PATRIOT Act, which expanded both surveillance and law-enforcement powers of the FBI, CIA, and the other U.S. security agencies.

Chapter Two

The Military-Industrial-Communication-Entertainment Complex

American power, expressed industrially, militarily, and culturally, has become the most potent force on earth [and] communications have become a decisive element in the extension of United States world power. . . . The technology of modern communications must be won away from its current custodians.

—Herbert Schiller, *Mass Communication and American Empire*, 206–7, 196[1]

This chapter details the main arguments of Schiller's *Mass Communications and American Empire*, first published in 1969, and explains the characteristic methods of research and writing evident in this work. To further explain Schiller's research and writing strategies, this chapter also draws from a book of collected essays Schiller coedited in this same period with Joseph D. Phillips, entitled *Super-State: Readings in the Military-Industrial Complex* (1970). Deconstructing, in the ordinary sense of that word, Schiller's concepts, method, and style makes useful procedures available for present-day power structure analysis of the political economy. Getting into the "Schiller method" helps us understand the connections of form and content in Schiller's writing as well as why *Mass Communications and American Empire* breathed life into the critical study of international communication and the political economy of communication and culture. In doing so, we come again to the biographical, in particular to how Schiller's contribution influenced a new generation of critical scholars in the 1970s.

Schiller's analysis has had tremendous holding power over forty years, and readers should find in the following account an astonishing degree of continuity with the present-day system that gives direction to what Schiller might have

29

called the military-industrial-communication-entertainment complex. Of course, the names of key political actors have changed, and with the end of the Cold War and the fall of Soviet Union, major reconfigurations of economic organization have modified not only the linkages in international power relations, but also altered the international division of labor in the communications and cultural area. Schiller accounts for these changes in a retrospective introduction to the second edition of *MCAE*, where he notes that "seismic shifts in the balance of world power have occurred since" the mid 1960s, but nevertheless "the preeminence of the American media/cultural sphere remains intact, if not more secure than ever" (*MCAE*, 1). He modified his earlier thinking to account for these real-world changes, a point that will be taken up in the conclusion.

Schiller elaborated his analysis of the information and communication component of American empire between 1965 and 1967, publishing some of this work in essays and articles in magazines such as *The Nation*, *The Progressive*, and *The Bulletin of Atomic Scientists*, as well as the *Administrative Law Review* and the *Antioch Review*. In 1968 he combined and extended the essays on this subject into a book-length study published the following year as *MCAE*. This was also the period in which Schiller acquainted himself with the dominant academic thinking in international communication research, which was represented in the 1960s by the pro-Western model of media and modernization, famously codified in Daniel Lerner's *The Passing of Traditional Society* (1958) and Wilbur Schramm's *Mass Media and National Development* (1964). Schiller's experiences in depression-era America, North Africa, and Germany brought him to question American moral authority in areas of political economic organization, and instilled in him respect for the "many places that might not accept [Schramm's] assumptions and would have other ways of organizing their societies" (quoted in Lent 1995, 153). Schiller's respect for non-Western cultural and historical experiences ensured that his writing would diverge from Schramm and others' work, which advanced the so-called dominant paradigm of communication research (*LNOC*, 107–26).

In addition to this internationalist and multiculturalist orientation, methodological differences also set Schiller's approach apart from the dominant communications paradigm. His method of researching international communication can to some extent be explained by his training and preferences in the study of economics, one that transposed resource and socioeconomic development theory into his thinking of communication–information. His general approach included both structural analysis of the largest governmental and corporate producers/users of information, as well as historical analysis documenting a conscious annexation of this resource by U.S. commercial and imperial forces around the world. Such questions had not been posed within communication

Herbert Schiller, University of Illinois, 1968.
Courtesy of the University of Illinois at Urbana-Champaign Archives. Record series number 39/2/26.

studies in quite as comprehensive a way as Schiller did. Perhaps it was for this reason that Schiller had difficulty finding an academic publisher who would take the manuscript. He ended up publishing the book with a small, one-man operation, Augustus M. Kelley, who dealt primarily in reprints of eighteenth- and nineteenth-century economics and philosophy texts. Only after its publication and eventual success did *MCAE* appear as an academic trade publication.

Schiller's goal in *MCAE* was to identify governing groups and their plans for communications, tracking the rise of commercial broadcasting in the United States after World War I and the post–World War II "envelopment of government communications facilities." He dissected the interlocking interests of corporate and military communications bureaucracies and explained how they attempted to spread the military-communications-entertainment complex via foreign and domestic policies and ideological campaigns. To this he added an analysis of the U.S. communication industry's television and film export component and the market pressures to internationalize the commercial system vis-à-vis efforts to use communications in national culture in the postcolonial regions. He demonstrated how communications technology, the newest at the time being satellite and cable, emerged from attempts to shore up the ruling system and extend U.S. strategic command over international communications. And finally he assessed how people in the United States and other countries have fared in their attempts to create a communications structure that diverged from official U.S. and corporate objectives.

To further understand how Schiller's analytical framework informed his writing style, a reading of the editors' introduction to *Super-State* is instructive. Schiller and Phillips' introductory essay begins with a title that asks, "The Military-Industrial Establishment: Complex or System?" Here, the complex and system were presented as two different models for understanding the military-industrial connection. The question was which was the more accurate model to use in the formulation of a policy that could significantly transform the military-industrial colossus. Before the question of reform could be answered, the problem of defining the military-industrial enterprise as a complex or a system had to be resolved.

Schiller used the word "complex" to name the institutional edifice of communications, electronics, and/or cultural industries. These formed variously into single complexes or were part of a larger complex. Throughout *MCAE* are references to the communications complex, the military-industrial complex, and the industrial-electronics complex. The permutations of "the complex" varied depending on the subject of analysis, but Schiller used the idea of the complex pretty consistently as a name for a real entity, "a bureaucratic colossus," as he and Joseph Phillips called it (1970, 25). Alternately, Schiller came to use the idea of "the system" to describe firmly established political economic relationships in which these bureaucracies were integrated. The system determines the range of operations and purposes of a particular complex. As we will see, the complex serves as a convenient term for understanding large organizations, their internal dynamics, and their interinstitutional relationships. A complex comprises entrenched bureaucracies in which the actors change over time while institutional roles and motivations remain largely the same. In that sense, the complex can capture in the shorter term the contemporary features of a particular power structure. In contrast, the notion of the system serves to describe the evolution of that structure over a much longer period. So, for example, universities and colleges in the United States can be described as a complex to illustrate the variety and hierarchy of occupations within them, the core decision-making groups, and the purposes and aims of curricula, technology, and budgets. But a decision to reduce the wage bill, fire instructors, and enlarge computing facilities, while appearing as an autonomous bureaucratic choice, is also a significant manifestation of the long-range priorities of system maintenance that postsecondary education in the United States serves.

The argument in *Super-State* begins with a critique of the commonplace view of the military-industrial complex as "an outgrowth of inadvertence rather than design" (Schiller and Phillips 1970, 25). If the complex were envisioned as a willy-nilly outcome of wartime empowerment of the armed forces followed by postwar overspending and further empowerment, then reform of the complex could be realized with a decisive intervention of political will. This was the sense given by President Dwight D. Eisenhower in his famous farewell address of 1961, where he shocked many listeners with his warnings that "we must guard against the acquisition of unwarranted influence, whether sought or unsought, by the military-industrial complex" (quoted in *Super-State*, 32). Virtually all of the essays in *Super-State* embraced this sense of the term as a colossal bureaucracy that was out of control and threatened to become too powerful—or, as conservative contributors saw it, as a figment of liberal intellectual musings. Whatever the case, the underlying assumption was that the military-industrial complex materialized in response to unforeseen historical circumstances.

However, if a complex were "regarded as organically inseparable from the political-economic structure that has evolved in the United States, a nodal link in *a powerful imperial system still extending its influence globally,* a very different perspective unfolds." That is, if the military-industrial links were deliberately forged in the creation of the imperial system, then the battle over reform of a complex "widens into a struggle for the survival of the System itself"—it "means going to the mat with the System itself" (Schiller and Phillips 1970, 26–27; emphasis in original). But to "go to the mat with the System" meant the analysis had to step beyond existing criticism of the military-industrial complex—at least as far as this criticism was represented by the informed opinion gathered in the *Super-State* essays—and ask what social force posed a fundamental challenge to the system.

Schiller and Phillips introduced the possibility of two challenges, one internal and one external to the United States-led system. The external challenge originated with socially progressive policies, socialist movements, and revolutions. Schiller and Phillips argued that such challenges were intolerable to the

U.S. leadership. As they put it, the continued existence of the U.S. dominance required

the continued existence of economies based on private property in the countries where [U.S. corporations] are located. Socialist revolutions must be prevented and, if possible, socialist countries must be converted to capitalism. To this end leading U.S. business circles have had a decisive part in the formulation of those policies on which the military-industrial complex is based. (Schiller and Phillips 1970, 25)

To meet this challenge, the U.S. leadership relied on an increasingly institutionalized "war budget" (defense budget) which, while being the primary means of defending the system against collapse globally and domestically, was also paradoxically the primary cause of internal instability within the American empire. The "military component is hardly a frill," they said, "if American capitalism expects to maintain its international position of dominance and its internal economic stability" (Schiller and Phillips 1970, 27). As they saw it, the allocations for the military-industrial complex would grow steadily to administer to systemic weaknesses while social allocations for education, health, and other life-enhancing programs (today we would include the environment) would suffer. Considering that they wrote during the height of the anti–Vietnam war movement, we can assume that Schiller and Phillips understood that such internal instabilities could lead to significant political challenges to U.S. imperialism.

In view of Schiller's understanding of the sweep of systemic forces, the calls for reforms of semiautonomous, bloated bureaucracies must have seemed to him naïve at best, deceptive at worst. We can see this thinking at work in the framing chapter of *Super-State*, but it comes to life much more fully in *Mass Communications and American Empire*. Schiller framed the subject of this book in historical terms to quickly build evidence showing the organic ties of the military-industrial-communications complex to the imperial American system. He challenged these designs of empire by countering them with examples of ways people from around the world have tried to use communication technology for positive social change rather than as cultural and infrastructural supports for U.S. imperialism. The book integrates the analysis of complex and system in the following way.

Chapter 1 shows the interdependence of complex and system in an historical account of the shift from British to American political and economic hegemony and the attendant build up of the communication complex to support the new imperial aspirant. It contradicts the empire deniers in government and academic circles who promoted the false idea that American influence was not merely nonterritorial, in contrast to the direct territorial imperialism of the

British Empire, but also benign and therefore unlike nineteenth-century imperialism.

Chapter 2 dresses down the celebratory histories of American commercial broadcasting. On one hand, Schiller assesses the for-profit system with an ironic attitude toward American self-admiration: "The development of broadcast communications in the United States affords perhaps the most damaging as well as the most recent evidence of how an exciting new possibility for human enlightenment and satisfaction can be transformed into a stultifying swamp by a web of retrogressive social institutions" (1992, 63). On the other hand, he shows why communication in the most developed country in the world does not offer an appropriate model for nations that were then considering the role communication might play in their own development. Advancements in U.S. communications came after U.S. industrial development, so there was no historical experience to show how U.S.-style commercialism could seriously work as a viable model for development communications (scolding Schramm, Lerner, and other "developmentalists" indirectly for making that assumption—we return to this issue in chapter 4). Furthermore, the government-endorsed market system in the U.S. "pushed radio communications first into the hands of equipment manufacturers and then into the arms" of the advertising-based commercial broadcast business (1992, 69).

Chapters 3 and 4 are almost entirely focused on "the complex," in this case, on interlocked features of the constituent bureaucracies in the military-industrial-communication colossus. Chapter 5 put this complex into perspective by looking at the systemic uses and functionality of the military-industrial-communication connection. Here the system is exemplified by the anticommunist (what were called counterinsurgency) strategies in American foreign policy and military action. Chapter 6 returns to complex analysis, this time to establish the significance of the U.S. television program and film export industry as both an economic and ideological force worldwide. Chapter 7 then reframes the complex to explain it in terms of the system's characteristic features, in this case the "spread of the American system, the commercial model of communications, to the international arena" (1992, 137). This prepares readers for fully integrated analyses of complex/system in the remaining chapters.

Chapter 8 examines efforts in the postcolonial world to become independent economically and culturally and suggests clear limitations in transposing import-substitution policies from manufacturing to communications. Import substitution created some foundation for modernizing yet-to-be-developed economies by barring foreign goods to create local manufacturing capabilities and markets for local goods. But Schiller argued that it doesn't work the same way in broadcasting. Governments considering analogous policies to create autonomous communications should be aware that they cannot physically prohibit broadcast content from crossing borders (as they could with manufactured goods), and that both foreign political powers and internal commercial forces can take advantage of this feature, as Schiller showed with historical examples from Europe and North America. Because of this, Schiller argued that only international charters can ensure autonomous development of national communications and cultural policy.

For example, if Canada chose to prohibit entertainment programming during weekday mornings to broadcast educational material for children, then U.S. broadcasters would have to agree to the same prohibition given the unstoppable spillover of American broadcast signals into Canadian airwaves. Similar examples could be applied worldwide where countries pursuing noncommercial systems bordered those with commercial systems. Without international agreements that respect different national ideas for using communications, he warned that official American support for commercialism, internal pressure of advertisers, and technological advances in space communications would combine to push all national communications complexes toward global homogenization. Chapter 9 focuses on the new satellite technology. Here Schiller provides a very detailed political history of how the United States took command of space communication with the establishment of U.S. corporate control of Comsat and Comsat's veto power within the international satellite consortium, Intelsat.

Finally, chapter 10 on "democratic reconstruction" proposes a transfer of communications to people who will use this technology for such socially productive ends as literacy, education, and cultural enrichment. Schiller holds out hope that American "under-groups" would be successful in their efforts to restructure American priorities so that the new international communications satellite system and cable technologies could be transformed into life-enhancing forces. The groups identified as being in a position to recognize alternative uses for the media included workers in the nonprofit, social service areas of health and education, disenfranchised university students and faculty, and activists in the "black social movement." The chapter warned against the seductions of tokenism, that is, the cooptation of dissenting views via token-offerings in the mass media that intermittently satisfied demands for progressive material, honesty, or reality in the overall menu of American broadcast entertainment. For Schiller, such tokenism had the effect of splintering organized resistance.

These arguments shattered the supposed transparency of international mass communication research, a newly emerging discipline whose leading representatives, Schramm and Lerner, had depicted communications technology as a benign force of modernization. Within a matter of pages, Schiller set up the book's overarching question of how the complex evolved to serve the "American Century," contradicting official and academic attempts to deny the existence of American imperialism. This argument drew on several works of economic historians and statements of political analysts to describe how the United States established its hegemony in the imperialist era and what the systemic requirements were for maintaining the number one position in the world. The book's manner of confronting the dominant paradigm was therefore by example rather than polemic. For instance, Schiller once cited Schramm's study of communication and national development, but then only to quote a United Nations Educational, Scientific, and Cultural Organization (UNESCO) cost estimate for the elimination of two-thirds of adult illiteracy worldwide—then about $1.9 billion dollars over a ten-year period. He borrowed the figure to invite his readers to rethink the proportional size of this huge budget to which most countries could ill afford to contribute then or now, noting that it was actually slightly less than the U.S. Department of Defense's yearly expenditure on telecommunications in 1967, or, paid out over ten years, "only ten percent of *one year's* budget allocation for U.S. military communications spending" (*MCAE*, 120). He thus showed that existing priorities for resource distribution, and the decision-making process that established those priorities, were fundamentally antidevelopment. But it was also a point of style that reflected how Schiller would regularly use conservative secondary sources in his research. Other citations plainly linked establishment thinking with people such as Ithiel de Sola Pool or Joseph Klapper, CBS researcher and promoter of the "limited effects" model of media power, by quoting their statements from a government committee report on the role of communication in American foreign policy.

Moreover, Schiller did not employ computational social science research methods, the established "objective" methods of the field. For the most part, he approached research methods—like econometrics, regression analysis, or survey research—wary of their utility to answer broad social questions. As Finnish communications scholar Kaarle Nordenstreng argued in a 1968 survey of American communication research, the prevalent American approach to communications suffered from "the general dilemma of positivism." Nordenstreng added that the "fact that certain aspects of reality lend themselves to convenient measure (and subsequent statistical elaboration) does not mean that these aspects are necessarily most essential to our understanding of reality" (Nordenstreng 1968, 215). Sharing this sentiment (Schiller knew Nordenstreng and his work at this point), Schiller did not follow the routine mass communications approach, dominated by behaviorist studies, but instead practiced an interpretive social science that allowed him to challenge the given conditions that "objective" American mass communication researchers traditionally accepted without question. *MCAE* thus inaugurated a new and unsparing critical discourse that challenged the authoritative representations of the American international communications model.

The way *MCAE* discussed communications must have been something of a shock to readers accustomed to the established mass communications literature. To a group of younger scholars, it was precisely this shock that alerted them to an alternative framework for analyzing their own research and observations of domestic and international mass communications. *MCAE* also stood out as a lone challenge to the futurism and utopian rhetoric that gilded communication studies literature at the time. Vincent Mosco, who would become a major figure in the field of political economy of communications, was a sociology graduate student at Harvard when he read *MCAE*. In the late 1960s and early 1970s, Mosco searched for writers who offered more critical approaches to the media than he was getting from his professors, Daniel Bell among them. Mosco "found Schiller's work unique for its political punch and engaging style" (Mosco 2001a, 191) and was taken with Schiller's confident analysis of the media component of U.S. imperialism and "struck by how alone he was among people writing for both an academic and wider public in the United States" (Mosco 2001b, 27). John Lent, who would also become a key contributor to critical political economy and international communication studies, also remembered how *MCAE* helped him to develop a theoretical framework for the research he had done in the mid to late 1960s on mass communications in the Philippines and the Caribbean. Like Mosco, Lent wanted to get to know Schiller and began to correspond with him. Lent recalled that his first exchange with Schiller in 1972 "made clear that this man had a number of exemplary qualities: humility, commitment to encouraging students and young scholars, a passion and devotion to critical scholarship, and an ability to fashion the right questions" (Lent 2001, 40).

John Lent and Vincent Mosco were among the many critical graduate students who learned of Schiller first through his writing and then—"On an off-hand chance that he might reply" (Lent 2001, 41)—through correspondence that sometimes included copies of dissertations and other writing. Schiller was indeed a remarkable correspondent, "the most assiduous letter writer I have known," as Frank Webster put it in his memoir of Schiller (Webster 2001, 33). His generous responses would offer a mix of comradely suggestions of method or perspective, a list of probing questions, and then his apologies for not having time to say or write more. These exchanges were like epistolary colloquia with Schiller, creating a virtual community of young and critical scholars that would help heighten Schiller's visibility in the field of communications. Throughout his career, it was "almost invariably at the insistence and under the auspices of graduate students and young faculty" that Schiller would be invited to speak at college campuses (quoted in Lent 1995, 142).

MCAE made perhaps an even more significant impact outside the United States. *MCAE* appeared at the right time and place, as international communications scholar Hamid Mowlana noted. Schiller "was writing exactly at the height of American dominance when the Third World nations and so called Non-Aligned Group of 77 were beginning to challenge U.S. policies in the post-colonial area" (Mowlana 2001, 23). Mowlana himself had been working on issues of communication and development in the late 1960s when he read *MCAE*, and found it useful in helping frame his study. Schiller and Mowlana's connection was typical of the group of communications scholars whose interests ranged beyond the system-serving provincialism of American communications research. For Mowlana, "What was so crucial about Herb's work at this time was that while many of us were thinking along the same lines, he was the one taking major steps to articulate and put it before the wider audiences of both students and faculty, not only in the United States but also in Europe and elsewhere" (Mowlana 2001, 21).

Mowlana was part of a community of internationalist scholars who formed a critical grouping within the International Association for Mass Communication Research (IAMCR—now the International Association for Media and Communication Research). Schiller became involved in the IAMCR in Herceg-Novi (Yugoslavia) in 1966, perhaps at the urging of Dallas Smythe, who was active in the organization. This is where Kaarle Nordenstreng, among others, also encountered Schiller for the first time (Nordenstreng 1993, 261fn). As Schiller grew closer to this group, his political-economic approach became more clearly identified with emerging debates within the international research community of the IAMCR and its collective projects and conferences. At the center of these debates was the effort to define and implement a new international informational system that corrected the imbalances caused by U.S. economic and cultural domination. By the end of the 1960s, the main forum for this critical reappraisal of the role of communication in world development was UNESCO, for which IAMCR acted as consultative research arm.

In 1969, UNESCO sponsored a "Meeting of Experts on Mass Communication and Society" in Montreal to discuss concerns of communication and information inequalities around the world (UNESCO 1969). Schiller was contacted by Dallas Smythe, who was at the meeting, and asked if he could send fifty copies of his book. Schiller never found out if anyone at the Montreal meeting actually read *MCAE*, but Kaarle Nordenstreng recalled the significance of Schiller's research in these meetings, to which Nordenstreng was also a major contributor. From that time forward Schiller became deeply involved in the theme of the UNESCO meeting: to push for a reorganization of global communications in order to create a more equitable system serving the informational and communications needs of the "have-not" countries.

The demands of the "have-nots" were being circulated not only via UNESCO efforts, but also through the Movement of Non-Aligned Nations, which began in 1955 in Bandung, Indonesia, to question the imperialist system from outside the structure of the West-East ideological conflict. By the late 1960s, calls for a new economic order to address these demands were matched by the calls for a new informational order. Schiller's writings, starting with *MCAE*, were considered by many to offer a solid theoretical and empirical grounding to advance the discussion of what came to be known as the New International Information Order (NIIO, later and more commonly known as the New World Information and Communication Order, or NWICO). As Tran Van Dinh put it, Schiller gave a clear explanation of the reasons "the nonaligned countries [were] starting the much delayed offensive against cultural imperialism" (1979, 264).

The disruptions in the imperial system that had provoked and inspired Schiller had influenced a broad range of intellectuals and activists around the world, many of whom Schiller would encounter at the IAMCR and the NWICO meetings. It was in this context that Schiller developed a number of additional projects in collaboration with Kaarle Nordenstreng and Dutch scholar Cees Hamelink. Although Nordenstreng had met Schiller in 1966 and got to know him better when he visited Schiller at Urbana in 1967 while on fellowship at Southern Illinois University, it was the collective work of defining a new international information order in the 1970s that increased their contact and mutual interests. The IAMCR fostered many such "intellectual alliances" with "critical communication scholars in Europe—Britain, Finland, Holland, and Eastern Europe," recalled Mowlana. But perhaps more important were the strong connections Schiller established "intellectually and emotionally with scholars, groups and individuals in post-colonial countries, especially in Latin America and Asia" (Mowlana 2001, 21). This formed a pattern of relationships that resulted in Schiller gaining greater recognition in the postcolonial regions than in the United States and in European intellectual circles. Eventually, so much of Schiller's work was translated (mostly into Spanish but also Russian, Arabic, Persian, Chinese, and others) that he became even "better known among the general public in non-Western countries" than in Western academia (Mowlana 2001, 24). Schiller also became very involved in the governance of the IAMCR organization in the 1970s, and was instrumental in opening up a research section concerned with the political economy of communication. Many younger scholars, such as Graham Murdock, first met Schiller in the mid-1970s through the political economy section meetings, which for nearly thirty years have continued to draw together the international community of critical political economists of communication and culture.

This chapter has shown how Schiller's work can serve as a manual on power structure analysis. The major works discussed here included *Mass Communications and American Empire* with reference to *Super-State: Readings in the Military-Industrial Complex*. Not discussed was another book that extended the themes and analysis, called *Triumph of the Image: The Media's War in the Persian Gulf—A Global Perspective*, an edited collection coordinated with George Gerbner and Hamid Mowlana in 1992. As the following chapters reveal, Schiller never abandoned the principal concerns of *Mass Communications and American Empire*, in particular issues of national communication policy, cultural imperialism, military-corporate enclosures around information, and postcolonial struggle. Likewise, his defiant style remained a refreshing counter to the celebratory depictions of U.S. material wealth and individualism pervading the media, a subject that occupied much of the analysis in chapters 6 and 7 of *MCAE*. We now turn to Schiller's sustained look at that ideological function of mass media, what he called "mind management."

NOTE

1. Page references are to the second edition, updated, Westview Press, 1992.

Chapter Three

Mind Management and the Shaping of the Informational Workforce

No cultural committee draws up secret instructions for the daily schooling and programming of the American people. . . . In truth, the process is much more elusive and far more effective because it generally runs without central direction. It is embedded in the unquestioned but fundamental socioeconomic arrangements that first determine, and then are reinforced by, property ownership, division of labor, sex roles, the organization of production, and the distribution of income. These arrangements, established and legitimized over a very long time, have their own dynamics and produce their own "inevitabilities." I have attempted to examine some of these inevitabilities and to question their legitimacy.

—Herbert Schiller, *The Mind Managers*, 5

Soon after Schiller returned to the United States in 1948, he became interested in how the general opinion in his home country could be so steeped in McCarthyite distortions about socialism and the capitalist system. How, he wondered, could his own thinking diverge from the mainstream as radically as it did? He asked what the mode was of inculcating public ideas and who organized it. What were the networks of dissemination? For various reasons, he did not return to these questions for twenty years, until *Mass Communications and American Empire*, when he began to articulate his ideas of how public knowledge could be produced and commandeered by profit-seeking interests in the military-corporate complex. In *MCAE*, this process was shown to extend throughout the international political economy, linking the informational apparatus to the fortunes of the West and the fates of poor and undeveloped regions. While *MCAE* contains descriptions of how domestic and international communications content shaped public consciousness, it does not present a complete framework for interpreting this process. It reveals only a first step in this analy-

sis, showing how the propertied class controlling the mass media was dedicated
to making the cultural environment more conducive to profit-making than to
education, public service, or other socially productive ends.

By the end of the 1960s, Schiller began to work on a full analysis of the
relation between informational control and public knowledge. In 1970, he
moved with his family to La Jolla, California, where he began to teach at the
University of California at San Diego. He was hired to establish a communications program at UCSD, and as "coordinator" he was encouraged to create a
media studies curriculum that explored the realities of media power. This
material grew into this period's major work, *The Mind Managers* (hereafter
TMM), published in 1973.

The idea for this book had been stewing for some time, but began to take
form after Schiller's intellectually prosperous shift into research on the communications component of American empire. His acknowledgements in *TMM*
recalled the efforts of his research assistants, librarians, and colleagues at the
University of Illinois in the preparation of the book. Schiller also acknowledged his debt to Dallas Smythe, who had pioneered the field in which the
concerns of *TMM* were first articulated and who would remain Schiller's long-
time friend, supporter, and link to other progressive communications researchers. The productive relationships he had at Illinois and with a growing number
of critical communications students and faculty around the world, not to mention the ferment of political activism of the 1960s, gave the initial impetus for
writing *TMM*. But it was the move to UCSD that would provoke the "unexpected and unconventional widening" of his thought that gave the final shape
to the book (*LNOC*, 36–38).

UCSD was planned in the 1950s and constructed in the 1960s on the Torrey
Pines Mesa atop the hills of northern La Jolla, a wealthy suburb built along and
above a few miles of rocky coves and sandy beaches north of San Diego, California. The UC regents had envisioned an elite school heavily geared to graduate study in science and technology, with some undergraduate teaching to help
pay for it. Its founders used the reputation of the Scripps Institution of Oceanography (SIO), financed by defense-related research since World War I, to
push in the 1950s for approval of a new UC college in the La Jolla area, where
some SIO faculty had bought thirty-eight acres of land to provide open housing in a zone that the La Jolla Real Estate Brokers Association had restricted to
white, Christian ownership. The rest of the land was provided freely by the
city and federal government, and by 1964, the new program in science and
engineering was opened at First College, later renamed Revelle College for
one of its founders. In 1965, a year in which a small group of UCSD students
protested the U.S. invasion of the Dominican Republic, the Marxist philoso-
pher Herbert Marcuse joined the faculty. In 1967, Second College opened,

later named John Muir College, extending an administrative initiative to enlarge the humanities curriculum. That year, the plans for a Third College were also approved (Gribble 2000).

Between 1967 and 1969, antiwar protests multiplied. By this time, Angela Davis, a Marxist writer, feminist, and an important figure in the Black liberation struggles in the United States, had arrived to study with Marcuse. Marcuse's twice-weekly Theories of Society lectures were becoming increasingly popular, filling lecture halls to capacity with students who wanted to learn more about Marxism and other philosophical advances that might help them understand the global conflicts and worldwide movement of students who fought for radical social change. This was not ignored by the conservative government of the period. Governor Ronald Reagan pressured the UC regents to censure the UCSD chancellor for allowing Herbert Marcuse to teach, especially to socialist intellectuals such as Davis, who was a well-known public figure and leading member of the Communist Party. Marcuse is said to have once shouted to the governor at a protest, "Mr. Reagan, you do not look very smart!" Whether this hit a nerve or not we can't know, but Marcuse was eventually forced to retire by a Reagan policy that placed age limits on faculty members, a policy that Reagan thought nothing of while serving as president past the age of seventy.[1]

Students won a greater say in academic governance of Third College by organizing throughout the late 1960s to stop the university's contribution to the devastating war in Vietnam. Using this influence, they were able to form strong coalitions that included Marcuse, Davis, and other activists. One of their goals was ensuring that plans for the new Third College be restructured to serve the higher education needs of blacks, Latinos, and Native Americans, and also that the new college be governed from below by deliberative democratic processes that included the participation of administrative staff, students, and faculty. In 1969, this coalition blocked the chancellor's offices, with the chancellor inside, and occupied Muir College, seizing buildings and asserting their demands. Among those demands was a call to end all defense-related research at UCSD and create socially productive programs using university resources, the centerpiece of which would be a radically different Third College than the one planned. Given this unrelenting political pressure and the general crisis of legitimacy institutions were suffering throughout the United States, the chancellor thought it best to agree to the reforms for Third College. But he did so without eliminating restrictive bureaucratic linkages between the new College's popular democratic organization and the rest of the university power structure.

Third College opened in 1970, at the height of this period of student activism, creative intellectual activity, and an apparent institutional commitment to academic freedom and participatory democracy. After Third College opened, protesters continued to pressure the administration to fulfill its promise to support an alternative curriculum for the new College. Also in that year, a student set himself on fire to protest the war, his death memorialized as a symbol of war's tragedy and the movement's commitment to end the university's supporting role in the war. This was the situation at UCSD when Schiller received his invitation to apply to head a new communications program. He recalled the appeal of the position:

> In this instance, the students, and some faculty sympathetic to their goals, were authorized to organize a curriculum for the new college. Four main areas were chosen for study: Third World studies; science and technology; urban and rural studies; and communication. Each was to focus on the special needs of the minority students. This domestic objective was of a piece with the Third World movement for a new international economic and information order, with local specifications. (*LNOC*, 36–37)

Schiller's attraction to this job was clear: it was the prospect of working to achieve the socially productive goals of the students rather than the institutional aims of the university bureaucracy, despite having to take on the usually unpleasant job of managing a new program. He was perfect for the position given his critical orientation and interests. First, however, he had to pass muster with student interviewers, which was, and is, a rare event in university governance. But he got the job, and the administration promised that the communications program would receive departmental status very quickly.

It did not. Part of the reason the program did not accede quickly to department status had to do with Schiller's inability to go along with administrative whims. The provost of Revelle College, in one bureaucratic episode, strongly recommended that Schiller hire a particular individual sight unseen—it turned out that this character was not only a communications professor with a mediocre record as a broadcast historian and teacher, but also one of the provost's old surfing buddies. Schiller said no. His obligation, as he understood it, was "to the new college and the students," not to his superiors' caprices. He would do as the students had asked, namely, "create a meaningful set of courses in the communication field that would enable those enrolled to develop their understanding and consciousness and overcome the mental servitude instilled in oppressed classes and groups" (*LNOC*, 37). The provost became associate chancellor for academic affairs within a year, a position from which he could manipulate the fortunes of Third College more directly, while Schiller spent more than a few years without a promotion, salary increase, or invitation to serve on important committees.

A full-fledged department would have had the autonomy to organize its curriculum and become the administrative home of its own faculty appointments. As it was, Schiller was only able to act as the "coordinator" of a program with three untenured faculty members assigned from other departments, though these included such creative and radical young scholars as Will Wright and Mark Lushington. For a very brief moment, however, these restrictions looked like they might ease up. In 1971, Schiller managed to wrangle two faculty positions fully appointed to the fledgling communications program. One of those jobs went to Michael Real, who had been active as the head of the Graduate Student Association at the University of Illinois, where he had worked on a committee with Schiller to organize students and faculty to pressure the university to eliminate their Reserve Officers' Training Corp (ROTC) program. Real finished his Ph.D. in communications soon after Schiller left for San Diego, letting Schiller know of his interest in a job. Real's work in critical theory and ritual aspects of communications eventually became central to American communications and cultural studies, especially in the area of media and sport.

Schiller was also able to appoint Oscar H. Gandy Jr. as a lecturer in the program. Gandy had received his M.A. from the University of Pennsylvania, where George Gerbner, a friend and former colleague of Schiller's at Illinois, had been Gandy's teacher. Gandy had been working at a local television station and became disenchanted with the rigid nature of the job, so when Gerbner advised him about the position in San Diego he was ready to make a move. After two years, Gandy went on to study for his Ph.D. at Stanford, and would eventually become a leading communications scholar writing on surveillance, critical political economy, race and communication, and interlocking interests in the government-corporate complex.[2]

Other critical scholars would follow throughout the 1970s and 1980s, often on a visiting basis. The list of visitors in the 1970s is alone impressive: Dallas Smythe, Joseph Phillips, Jeremy Tunstall, Nicholas Garnham, Tapio Varis, Kaarle Nordenstreng, Vinnie Mosco, among others. But the meager support from the administration remained stagnant for many years, and UCSD several times came close to terminating the program altogether until it was reorganized in the 1980s under new, and better funded, management who gave the program a more "scientific" look. The program survived until then as a result of the growing popularity of the courses that students believed connected with their own media-saturated lives.

Schiller's vibrant teaching style became quickly known among UCSD students. Many students who signed up for his courses out of curiosity were soon drawn to the study of communication after an inspiring Schiller lecture. In his larger introductory courses, he would speak engagingly about history, major world events, and the developing importance of communication. In one session, students could hear of the development of the railroad, telegraph, telephone, and wireless radio as these served different periods of capitalist development, from the nineteenth-century era of the Robber Barons, to the emergence of U.S. imperial aspirations and growing naval power, to the rise of monopoly capitalism, corporate media, and the corporate-state complex. In another he might return to a premodern period of technological development to draw attention to the collaborative social bases of innovation in order to illustrate how technology was a social construct, and also to refute the present-day emphasis on individual creativity and ingenuity that hides social processes underlying technological change. And in still another, he would give a sweeping historical presentation explaining the role of labor in agricultural, industrial, and finally in the emerging knowledge industry of the so-called information age.

His courses showed how messages were delivered, how to interpret their form and meaning, and how audiences were organized to understand them. Typical assignments included the appendix to George Orwell's *1984* on the "Principles of Newspeak" and excerpts of Sergei Eisenstein's *Film Sense*, among others. He examined how messages circulated in ordinary and routine ways via film, publishing, television, radio, tourism, recording, advertising, public relations, the press, and so on. His approach was not focused on the individual formats and genres, or on the aesthetic and emotional responses peculiar to each. Instead, he attempted to approach varied material as a whole to find a consistent meaning across media forms. As he put it in *TMM*:

> A study of TV, radio, or film products would reveal, I am convinced, a similar, if not identical, pattern. For, despite Marshall McLuhan's insistence on each medium's uniqueness, there is an underlying similarity in the message flow with respect to basic systemic values. It is not, as McLuhan claims, that the "medium is the message," but that *all the media transmit the same message*, each in its own form and style. . . . Their formats and the reactions they generate are worlds apart. What can be noted and compared, however, are the social messages interspersed in each. (81)

In the classroom, Schiller would make connections between the social messages emanating from the media–communication complex and the wider political economy by a simple demonstration, which became another signature style he employed in many public lectures. He would reach into the pocket of his tweed jacket and pull out an article or two that he had recently clipped from a newspaper. From that small clipping he would begin to talk at length about "what it reported, how it reported it, and what was left out or distorted," linking this analysis to the broader history of the communications complex and corporatization of the "knowledge factory" (*LNOC*, 37).

The British sociologist Frank Webster, whose writing on information technology has been inspired by Schiller's work and friendship, sat in on many of these lectures when he was a guest professor at UCSD in the early 1980s. He remembered how "students in that audience, one that was always large . . . were transformed by the man whom they called 'the discovery of UCSD.' They will have learned passion, engagement, and alternative visions, those critical faculties that universities so often proclaim is their goal but so rarely actually provide" (Webster 2001, 32).

Schiller's love of teaching contributed to the program's reputation among students, and enrollments eventually "exceeded those of most of the traditional departments. This guaranteed our survival," Schiller said, "since the university has become no less a retailer in need of 'customers' than any department store" (*LNOC*, 38). Even as the numbers grew, the administration's lack of confidence would not fade. Michael Real assumed the position of coordinator during his second year in the program after it became clear to Schiller that the administration was not going to fulfill its promises, while Schiller accepted invitations to visit Finland and the Netherlands. The following year, when Schiller was on leave to teach in Amsterdam, the administration put the assistant vice chancellor in charge of the department. Oscar Gandy had seen little hope in this setting and, by 1973, was easily drawn away to complete his graduate studies at Stanford. By the mid 1970s, the department officially had three and a half full-time faculty and over three hundred majors, who were unable to actually list communications as their major because of the (imposed) precarious status of the program. Students would instead receive diplomas that said they had majored in cognate fields, such as visual arts. There were no official bachelors degrees awarded wholly in communications until a decade later, when the program curriculum was reorganized and communications received departmental status.

Communications in the 1970s was still pretty much a new discipline with a fragile identity everywhere in the nation—there were very few Ph.D.s in communications, and most departments in the United States were comprised of faculty from traditional fields such as sociology, political science, linguistics, speech and rhetoric, history, visual arts, theater, and English (UCSD did not hire anyone with a communications Ph.D. after Michael Real until the 1990s, when Dan Schiller joined the faculty). So, as Schiller said, "Across the university, communication was regarded as a subject lacking substance." Moreover, because Schiller's courses examined the actual power structure and realities of media control, the program was said to be run by ideologues, as if "no established discipline would admit to the slightest possibility that its field might have an ideological slant" (*LNOC*, 38). At the time, only literature, visual arts, and perhaps urban studies had the same sort of reputation for having radical faculty (sociology had a few younger scholars on the left, who counted Aaron Cicorel as one of their and Third College's major supporters, but for the most part it

Herbert Schiller, University of California at San Diego, 1971.
Courtesy of Scripps Institution of Oceanography Archives. SIO negative number M-3646–27.
Copyright University of California Regents.

was a very conservative department). Still, none of these were stigmatized by Red-baiting to the extent that communication was. There were also external promoters of this caricature, for instance, the "two nationally syndicated columnists, Roland Evans and Robert Novak," wrote that Schiller was "a white radical brought in to mold the minds of minority students"—an assertion steeped in the racial stereotype that students of color were like "malleable clay, waiting to be shaped by manipulative fingers" (*LNOC*, 38). In response to this combination of local forces and intellectual interests, Schiller set out to write a book that would directly contribute to the goals of Third College students and establish a clearer identity for the critical communications discipline that had been tarnished by misrepresentations circulating on and off campus at the time.

We can thus understand Schiller's overall approach to the subject matter in *The Mind Managers* as intentionally organized for teaching students engaged in political activism and historical change, such as those at Third College. The book speaks to readers who have a deep desire to challenge the media, information, and cultural sources that promote subservience to systemic goals. Consider the influence the Third College students must have had on Schiller's idea for this book. In addition to gaining limited involvement in university governance, the students had also demanded definitional power to name their college after two heroes of national liberation: Patrice Lumumba, the anti-imperialist Congolese prime minister who was murdered in a 1961 coup d'etat aided by the CIA, and Emiliano Zapata, the Mexican revolutionary leader. Clearly, students who thought of their school as the Lumumba-Zapata College were concerned with the workings of empire, were committed to social justice, and were eager to hear dissenting perspectives that helped them articulate their opposition to the escalating war in Vietnam.

It should not be surprising, therefore, to read in the first few pages of *TMM* an endorsement of the ideas of Paolo Freire, whose radical pedagogy insisted that the learning environment offer a liberatory education that builds on the students' experience of social problems and the concrete reality of their existence. Education was supposed to awaken students to their historical role so that they no longer remain subject to manipulation, or mind management, as Schiller phrased it in his introduction. In this sense as well, Schiller's early experience of the academic enterprise resonated in his critique of the knowledge industry, especially in the sections of *TMM* that analyze the educational and "para-educational" apparatus comprised by large public sector information providers and private cultural industries.

TMM offered readers a learning experience that stood in opposition to the dominant university curriculum. It addressed readers not merely as students, however, but as agents within the social structure who would join the ranks of educated labor one day. If Schiller's readers could comprehend the structural changes in the labor market—which was then enticing them with increasing numbers of information-related occupations—and link that understanding to what was being attempted by the information-communications sector, then he would have provided what his students' generation had demanded. This was incidentally the generation of his own children, to whom, along with their friends, the book was dedicated.

So Schiller chose to make the consciousness of social labor the focus of his systemic analysis, and framed his accounts of the military-industrial-communication-education complex accordingly. In each chapter, Schiller began with or eventually interpreted mind management as it affected the various groups who would be joining the growing ranks of "knowledge workers" required by the expanding informational apparatus. What was taught, who was providing learning material, what were the pervasive messages, what were the methods of inculcation—these were the questions underlying the way *TMM* documented the attempts of capitalist enterprises, military powers, and government coordinators to produce a labor force that would serve the needs of an advanced, high-technology industrial state.

Schiller argued further that the "para-educational" and military-government ensemble became mind managers in an attempt to disarm this workforce's critical ability to question militarism, consumerism, market criteria, or the love of technology promoted in popular culture and academia. Schiller contended that disruptions in the system caused by a growing population of students critical of the status quo—that unruly generation widely seen as constituting future managing groups—provoked a number of structural changes in the information-communication-cultural complex. And, as these disruptions joined the wider world-historical movement against imperialism and U.S.-style commercialism, the reactionary escalation of mind management spread to an international scale.

The book thus begins by orienting the reader toward critical insight about the learning process itself. Chapter 1 addresses a reader who sees him or herself as resistant to manipulation, but who must nevertheless be watchful of the conditions for manipulation. Schiller identified two sets of conditions for successful manipulation, the first comprising five interrelated beliefs or myths (*TMM*, 8–24).

At the top of the list was *the myth of individualism*, which gave people a false sense of their disconnection from the social world and promoted the idea that freedom was a personal, and not a collective, matter. According to this myth, the independent mind could not be controlled, personal freedom of choice defined life's direction, and private ownership of property was the ultimate expression of individualism and the greatest form of freedom. The promoters of the modern corporation depended on the persistence of this myth to justify their operations, however harmful these were.

Next was *the myth of neutrality*, or the idea that the operations of power are transparent. This myth flowed from the first, for if the mind was independent and free from manipulation, then it followed that key social institutions (the presidency, Congress, the judiciary, etc.) would not dare, even if they could, deceive the public. The people would know. The myth that governmental power is transparent, ideologically neutral, and merely pushing paper also fosters belief that the leadership is beyond reproach and suspicion. There are no vested interests behind the scenes—you vote for the person, not an established system of powerful interests. And if the independent mind is sovereign and can truly see the workings of government, then when propaganda, bias, and prejudice occur they fool no one. If this is so, dissenting opinion can be ignored (marginalized by the media) as needless, mindless, or just redundant.

Third is *the myth of unchanging human nature*, which presupposes that existing social arrangements are the result of some natural (or divine) process, and are therefore beyond human intervention. Basic relationships, even aggression, avarice, poverty, class, and war can be explained by this myth of fixed human nature. The potential for social change simply doesn't exist.

The myth that human progress occurs without social conflict is next. This myth renders historical struggles against racism or clashes between worker and owner as unintelligible, except as problems between individuals who just can't get along, ensuring the status quo won't be disrupted by demands for justice. In order to propagate the myth that social conflict is nonexistent, evidence of structural inequality has to be erased from the cultural curriculum (news, schooling, entertainment, etc.). Further, the successes of social struggle (the eight-hour day, the weekend, medical benefits, etc.) have to be presented as the result of consensual arrangements rather than as outcomes of class conflict.

And finally *the myth of media pluralism* gives a false sense that the multiplication of television channels and other media outlets guarantees informational diversity and competing opinions. "The fact of the matter," argued Schiller, "is that, except for a rather small and highly selective segment of the population who know what they are looking for and can therefore take advantage of the massive communication flow, most Americans are basically, though unconsciously, trapped in what amounts to a no-choice informational bind" (*TMM*, 19).

Schiller argued that people rely on these myths for making sense of the world because of two dominant techniques for information delivery. These techniques form the second set of conditions for mind management. One technique is *the constant interruption of thought* that typifies the commercial media environment, from television's chronic advertising hiccups to the distracting shopping landscape of most American cities. This fragmentation of ideas and expressions mirrors the general trend to atomize information and compartmentalize these bits into separate departments of knowledge—a feature of the educational system itself. Such fragmentation makes it hard for people to take a holistic view of society and see the links between politics, economy, and culture. The second technique is devoted to real-time delivery of information presented in *non-stop informational flows without pause for ethical, historical, or political reflection.* The techniques of constant interruption of thought and nonstop flows of information were formal qualities of a technology that were intentionally built to ensure political passivity among recipients. In Schiller's words:

> Though most of these entertainments demand nonparticipation, in the physical sense at least, there is nothing inherent in radio, television, or film—to take the most important of the popular recreational arts—that inevitably and exclusively creates mental torpor. . . . The main point [is] that the *aim* of television and radio programming and films in a commercial society is not to arouse but to lessen concern about social and economic realities. (*TMM*, 30)

Once Schiller explained these conditions for manipulation in chapter 1, he was ready to move on to the manifestations of mind management in the "informational arts," which he elaborated in different contexts throughout the book. Before examining how he did this, consider the themes of the remaining chapters of *The Mind Managers.*

Chapter 2 focuses on the transformation of government knowledge-information production that accompanied the growth of government public relations and executive secrecy, both of which functioned to determine the quality of available information while providing an oversupply of junk information.

Chapter 3 shows how the military-corporate complex influences educational resource allocation in the form of government support for corporate models and commercial control over public education.

Chapter 4 details ways that entertainment and recreational businesses expose people to the persistent system-serving message that entertainment is politically neutral.

Chapter 5 shows how polling and survey research work as techniques of control that organize audiences and public knowledge.

Chapter 6 tracks the internationalization of commercialism and the increased presence and importance of the global market research that followed capital flows and attendant multinational advertising.

Chapter 7 explains why the knowledge-information's elevation within the economy brought about a social contradiction: as "knowledge work" skills and resources spread so do new abilities to question the system. Information controllers reacted by promoting deficient and fragmentary information on the commercial side, and by replacing vital information with manipulative public relations and advertising techniques in the electoral process and throughout government branches and departments. When people proved that they were not dupes, more intense mind management was ordered up.

Chapter 8 argues that the "new media" (then cable television with interactive prospects of broadband uses) could not alone bring about the much needed democratization of American society; new forms of activism using smaller and more affordable communications technology were the best defense against information control and mind management.

The method Schiller employed in *The Mind Managers* was the same as the one he developed in *Mass Communications and American Empire*. The accounts of various complexes and systemic connections continue to regulate the flow of descriptions, analysis, and interpretation. The primary and secondary sources also follow the pattern set out in *MCAE*, although there was more emphasis on secondary analytical sources in television studies, including prominent places for the critical opinions of Erik Barnouw, the progressive broadcast historian, and Les Brown, the industry analyst, as well as the international research of Alan Wells, who edited a number of critical readers in media studies during the 1970s. In this sense, *TMM* showed Schiller's ongoing investigations into the discipline itself, with a particular interest in the perspectives that offered some critical insight rather than a celebration of the mass media and cultural industries. Fred Friendly, former head of CBS news and collaborator with Edward R. Murrow, was cited in this vein, as were commentaries by Harold Lasswell and cultural journalist Richard Schickel. And finally, Schiller incorporated more insight from Marxist media criticism and cultural studies, including works by Rudolph Arnheim, Raymond Williams, Armand Mattelart, and Ariel Dorfman on the impact of media manipulation serving U.S.-led commercialism in Europe and Latin America.

TMM brushes elbows with the so-called dominant paradigm in communications research. But again, as in *MCAE*, Schiller did not confront the fundamental principles or leading theorists of this work directly or explicitly. Rather, the critique was implicit in Schiller's argument that survey research and polling, which share a methodological foundation with dominant communications research, evolved as methods of social control—surveys and polls categorize people in order to manage populations and organize public knowledge, consumption, and media use for systemic ends. "To take a poll is itself an act of social policy," Schiller wrote. "To inquire about a group's views, for *any* reason, suggests the initial mind-set of the poll-taker and implies a promise of future action or, no less significantly, inaction, somewhere in the societal decision-making apparatus" (*TMM*, 105). Schiller tracked the evolution of survey techniques within the military-industrial complex and demand-side of war-related research, offering a simple but convincing demonstration that contradicted the two main claims of the survey research industry—namely, that polling is a feedback loop between decision-makers and the public, thus serving democratic ends, and that it produces objective facts about people and their preferences. According to Schiller, "polls have served democratic ends not poorly but disastrously. They have cultivated a deceptive guise of neutrality and objectivity. They have fostered the illusion of popular participation and freedom of choice to conceal an increasingly elaborate apparatus of consciousness manipulation and mind management" (*TMM*, 123). Here Schiller offered a prescient critique of the opinion survey as the means by which commercial and government leaders would eventually and zealously come to organize their public relations efforts and defend their positions against public criticism (see Lewis 2001).

TMM provided substantial accounts of the workings of the military-industrial complex similar to those in *MCAE*. Here the focus was on the government component of the knowledge industry and the government enclosures around information resulting, for example, from the reorganization of the executive branch in the 1960s with the expansion of White House staff advisors who collected information and generated policy. Schiller documents the increasing frequency with which so-called advisors claimed executive privilege in order to withhold information vital to public assessment of government activities. For example, *TMM* documented one episode in which Donald Rumsfeld, current defense secretary, withheld information from Congress on cost of living conditions in the United States in 1972 in the name of executive privilege while serving the Nixon White House—where Dick Cheney, current U.S. vice president, also worked as a high-level staff member. In this analysis, Schiller was able to take the shifts of policy within the government bureaucracy, including the exemptions in the Freedom of Information Act (FOIA), and show how the lockdown on information served to limit public awareness of the extent of activities taking place in the imperial system. The FOIA exemptions, for instance, allowed the government to withhold from the public information directly related to "the war machine, foreign policy decisions affecting the empire, corporate practices [related to trade secrets], and resource decision-making" related to mining, oil exploration, and efforts related to geological and geophysical data (*TMM*, 57).

Schiller also documented the trend toward privatized educational enterprises, as government relinquished much of its responsibility to educate the American people. Here the emphasis was on the hype around educational technology and programs based on "performance contracting," in which regimented training substituted for learning, and skills serving military and business replaced substance serving an informed democracy. Again, Schiller offered a forward-looking critique of the restructuring and privatization of public education in the United States, a process that continues today to be led by the promise of computer-based teaching aids, charter schools (today's "performance contractors"), and a government leadership complacently starving public education.

In sum, Schiller questioned the existing cultural curriculum and interpreted the aims and preferences of the forces defining that curriculum as attempts to control the worldview of the next generation of knowledge workers, their habits of consumption, and their political disposition toward the established order. As long as he focused on large, relatively enclosed bureaucracies, or large institutional ensembles held together by common market criteria, Schiller was able to draw together sufficient evidence of a pattern of decision-making to show systemic connections, just as he had in *MCAE*. But an interesting comparison between *TMM* and *MCAE* draws attention to a conceptual modification Schiller had to make when analyzing the complex of private cultural industries from which people derived most of their everyday exposure to the apparatus of mind management. There were many disconnected commercial enterprises offering diverse products that nevertheless carried similar meanings, for example, value preferences and political perspectives that reproduced the myths outlined above. However, the method he used did not show interlocking financial, organizational, or sectoral commitments that linked such diverse corporations as TV Guide, Disney, and National Geographic. What he did show was that, while they may not have shared leadership or direction, they did have ideological ties to one another. That is, they formed a community of common interests, despite superficial differences. By sticking to the analysis of their shared ideological function, Schiller could only suggest actual institutional links, leaving for his and other's future research the task of detailing internal dynamics that link these operations to military-corporate leadership. Nevertheless, the argument's strength was in showing how the cultural environment of future "knowledge workers" became saturated by interpretations of life that were congenial with the values and the systemic goals of foreign policy, consumerism, and militarism.

The influence *TMM* had on younger scholars has already been mentioned, but it is worthwhile to note that among the themes developed in the book several have served as starting points for deeper analysis. The general introduction to manipulation joined with an already well-established body of critical theory and criticism of the mass society, especially the work of German scholars such as Marcuse and others from the Frankfurt School, including Theodor Adorno and Max Horkheimer, as well as younger writers such as Hans Magnus Enzensberger, whose very similar work, *The Consciousness Industry,* appeared in English translation a year after *TMM*, though its main essay, "The Industrial-

ization of the Mind," appeared originally in 1962. These works formed a powerful reading list for courses on cultural analysis and criticism throughout the
1970s and 1980s, and still appear in course materials today. Michael Parenti is
another writer who has continued to develop media criticism similar to Schiller's own by applying ideological analysis of television and film in a critique of
American empire.

In contrast to many of these writers, however, Schiller was explicit about his
support for emerging forces of resistance, including video activists who wanted
to challenge the system. He discussed these activists in the concluding chapter
of *TMM*, along with a number of possibilities and limitations they might face
in their work. This attention to alternative media practices created close relationships for Schiller in the video activist community, and led to his collaborations in the 1980s with DeeDee Halleck and the Paper Tiger TV video
collective, which developed a show called "Herb Schiller Reads *The New York
Times*."

Schiller's very unique work on the military-industrial enclosures around
communication and information would be further developed by Schiller himself during the 1980s, especially the military component. By the 1980s, however, he was not alone, and an important group of younger writers—including
Vincent Mosco, Janet Wasko, Kevin Wilson, Dan Schiller, Frank Webster,
Kevin Robins, and Bill Melody, among other scholars—were already making
significant contributions to the political economy of communication and
information. Schiller also developed his ideas on the information economy in
a number of important works in the 1980s and 1990s. This period of writing
will be taken up in detail in chapter 5. The industry ownership analysis that
remained somewhat underdeveloped in *TMM* would be complemented
greatly by work carried out by Robert McChesney, Edward Herman, and
Thomas Guback and his students. Though *TMM* certainly contributed much
to the framework for understanding the larger strategic position and function
of media corporations, Schiller did not give the same quantity of detail to the
ownership analysis of the three media corporations (Disney, TV Guide, and
National Geographic) as he did to other aspects of the communications complex, in particular military and political leadership.

Schiller's analysis also focused on the strategic role marketing research played
in the extension of the values and assumptions of the corporate-cultural conglomerates. He noted the defining role marketers were playing in the content
of messages produced in television and film. Following *The Mind Managers*,
Schiller's United Nations Educational, Scientific, and Cultural Organization
(UNESCO) report, *Communication Follows Capital* (1979), showed the over-
whelming impact of advertising on all commercial media content. Unfortu-
nately, this commissioned report became, as Nordenstreng argues, a "hostage

of high politics" at UNESCO, which refused to publish it in a fit of "anti-intellectual repression" in the 1970s (1993, 252–53). Other significant work on this theme includes Armand Mattelart's *Advertising International* (1991) and work by Wyatt (1995), and Miller et al. (2001)—this research tracked the trends of advertising and marketing influence in the global film and television industries identified in *TMM*. Another significant area of work that built on these themes would be carried out by Oscar Gandy Jr., in articles and a book, *The Panoptic Sort* (1993), in which Gandy developed a rich analysis of the growing surveillance component in the political economy of information, expanding the study of marketing research as a form of social control and discrimination.

Schiller enjoyed a growing number of productive relationships with colleagues around the world in the 1970s. For example, he and Dallas Smythe collaborated on projects, in particular a noteworthy report and analysis of the state of the media in Chile under the Popular Unity government led by President Salvador Allende (1971–1973) (Schiller and Smythe 1972). In this assessment of the Chilean *proceso* that was socializing the wealth of the nation and enlivening civil society, they noted the anomaly of the privately held communications apparatus. By nationalizing other industries, and curtailing the manipulative appeals of advertising, the Popular Unity party had created a situation in which large media holdings were being starved of their traditional sources of revenue. Advertising agencies were closing, practically erasing demand for marketing research. Schiller and Smythe showed the close ties of the information controllers and the industrial interests whose holdings had been nationalized, raising the question about how a free-market policy for media control risked giving these powerful groups a propaganda arm to wage a war of words, and eventually tanks, against Allende. They concluded with a hopeful vision for the socialist *proceso*, adding that "the extent to which the media are used by the people and for the people will be decisive in the safeguarding of what has already been achieved" in Chile (1972, 61). The Allende government was overthrown in a bloody coup d'etat the following year, helped by the privately held media's massive propaganda effort that the CIA aided under orders from President Nixon, Secretary of State Henry Kissinger, and U.S. military leadership (Landis 1975; Hitchens 2001).

Writing about Chile initiated subsequent occasions for Schiller's contact with Latin American researchers, including Rafael Roncagliolo, Osvaldo Sunkel, Fernando Reyes Mata, Juan Somavia, Noreen Janus, Enrique Gonzalez Manet, and others. This was a time of much travel and teaching, adding to an already great number of yearly journeys for the Schillers. Schiller also got to know Armand and Michèle Mattelart and their work on cultural imperialism and popular struggle, very important themes that moved to the center of Schiller's thinking at this time. The year *The Mind Managers* was published, Schiller was on leave from UCSD, working as a visiting professor at the University of Amsterdam and the University of Tampere (with Nordenstreng, Varis, and others) and lecturing at various universities throughout Scandinavia. The following chapter focuses on this eventful period of writing when Schiller devoted himself to analyzing the cultural supports of political and economic imperialism and became more deeply involved in efforts to devise communications-cultural policies that could transform the existing system of mind management.

NOTES

1. See also *Herbert's Hippopatamus*, Paul Alexander Juutilainen's movie about Marcuse and this period of UCSD history, accessible online at Douglas Kellner's Illuminations web site, at www.gseis.ucla.edu/faculty/kellner/Illumina%20Folder/marc.htm (accessed May 5, 2003).

2. In 1987, Gandy joined the faculty at the University of Pennsylvania's Annenberg School of Communication. In 1998, he was granted an endowed professorship in information and society through the Annenberg Public Policy Center. When asked to come up with a name for the chaired professorship during the term of his occupancy, Gandy decided he would like the position to be known as the Herbert I. Schiller Term Professor in Information and Society.

Chapter Four

Cultural Imperialism and the Limits to National Communications–Cultural Policy

The attainment of critical consciousness is not an ultimate destination, but an ongoing process whose unfolding will continually surprise and confound patterns of thought and habit that prevail at each point along the historical road of human development. Current efforts at communications-cultural policy making must be seen and understood in this way. However advanced or primitive the formulations may be, they are only markers on an endless road to the realization of human potential.

—Herbert Schiller, *Communication and Cultural Domination,* 96–97

Schiller wrote what became his most influential monograph, *Communication and Cultural Domination,* between 1973 and 1975 (hereafter *CCD*). Published in 1976, this book revisits Schiller's lifetime concerns with the devastating effects that accompany the globalization of the capitalist class system. In that sense, Schiller extended his interpretation and critique of the international political economy begun in preparation of *MCAE.* What distinguished this masterful synthesis from his first two books was its outline of a theory of cultural imperialism, which Schiller offered as a model of "basic relationships that structure power domestically and internationally" (*CCD,* 4). As we will see, Schiller began to modify his assessment of the cultural component of imperialism in the 1970s largely as a result of his new research and experiences shared within a community of critical international writers and activists. As he moved from the comparatively solitary research of the mid 1960s into a more collective dynamic in the mid to late 1960s, thanks in part to Dallas Smythe's continuing support, mediation, and encouragement, Schiller's analysis of cultural imperialism became at once more explicit and more closely tied to a series of organized efforts to challenge the existing imperial system and the information-communication apparatus supporting it.

His participation in the International Association for Mass Communication Research (IAMCR), beginning in the mid 1960s, introduced him to a "friendly forum" that offered an ethos of "internationalism" that Schiller found "enormously self-sustaining" (*CCD*, ii). In addition to the academic debates generated within IAMCR, he also contributed directly and (indirectly through his writings) to a series of UNESCO efforts to define a new international information order. He became involved with many international gatherings and research projects in the 1970s, including UNESCO's International Commission for the Study of Communication Problems (named the MacBride Commission for its chairman). In addition, and perhaps most importantly, the early 1970s saw a proliferation of efforts by many national states to formulate national communications and cultural policy. This was a novel but fraught issue on the international political agenda. The struggles around these attempts to formulate policy became extremely significant for Schiller, who began to question the forces promoting policy agendas, as well as the prospects for such policy in the international system that he had analyzed. One of the most pressing problems, as he saw it, was the threat that entrenched policy discourses posed to the democratic formulation of new national communication policies.

CCD was Schiller's answer to these questions. It is important to note at the outset that *CCD* does not simply outline the cultural imperialism thesis, as many commentators have understandably suggested, but rather presents a thesis of resistance to cultural imperialism. This was Schiller's contribution as a public intellectual to the ongoing deliberations over how to formulate a communication and cultural policy within or against the imperial system. The "within or against" (my words) is also significant, for Schiller assumed that the Western model of commercial communications may in fact be preferred by policymakers in many nations, though he insisted that adopting it without understanding its consequences could be fatal. In this context he introduced the important questions of who makes national policy and if there were self-interested political alignments between those national decision-makers and the centers of power in the United States.

Thus, a major part of this book returns to the United States' experience as an historical and empirical example of what nations might expect should they opt for the American arrangement. Schiller wouldn't say there was an officially recognized model or policy discourse in the United States, but instead introduced an important concept to describe the tacit policy guiding the American communications-cultural complex: *institutionalized communication domination* (*CCD*, 81)—a notion we examine in more depth below as we explore the major themes of this work.

First, another general introductory comment has to be made. *CCD* marked a change in stylistics and method from Schiller's earlier work. Here, Schiller writes in a more openly sardonic tone when discussing the self-serving claims made by academic and government sources—this tone actually conveyed an approximate sense of his speaking style more than his writing generally allowed. But he also developed his conceptual positions respectful of scholarly antecedents, and in doing so explicitly endorsed specific writers (including Nicholas Garnham, Raymond Williams, and Stuart Hall) from the fields of critical communications and cultural studies, fields that were quickly expanding in the late 1960s and early 1970s. In addition, there was a more apparent influence of critical international work, largely drawn from researchers associated with the IAMCR (John Lent, Elizabeth Fox, Luís Ramiro Beltrán, Rita Cruise O'Brien, Mowlana, Nordenstreng, Garnham, and others). Of course, Schiller still relied on his tried and true methods of "listening in" to power-wielders and decision-makers and using sources familiar to us from the earlier works: mainstream press accounts, government documents, testimonies of government representatives, and so on.

Finally, as policy questions are also discursive questions, Schiller paid more attention than in the past to deconstructing the writing of leading members of the dominant international communications research enterprise. In this case, we find a critique of William Read's economism, but more importantly Schiller directly confronted the work of Daniel Lerner and, especially, Ithiel de Sola Pool. Schiller's abiding concern with informational resource distribution for equitable socioeconomic development led to his critical assessment of U.S. domination in international communication, but here he added a critique of the academic entrepreneurs who rented their intellectual support to U.S. foreign policy via "objective" and "scientific" studies on the positive economic outcomes of the "free flow of information" and information technology transfers. It follows that he would perceive efforts to formulate national communication and cultural policy in terms of political and social struggle rather than as the expert, technocratic application of models that lead to system modernization, especially when those models purport to expand freedom of expression by furthering the commercial enclosures around informational resources. This was Schiller's main criticism of Pool's work, which he felt promoted an elitist and professionalized technological solution to social ills with a view of technology as a benign or neutral instrument for creating conditions of modern democracy. In working through this critique of technological determinism, Schiller elaborated perhaps his clearest statement thus far on technology's socially constructed characteristics.

Similar to our preceding discussions, this chapter outlines the main points in *CCD* and traces some of the temporal links of this period to new collaborations, some mentioned already, and to the community of younger scholars. At the conclusion of this chapter, we explore possible modifications of the cultural imperialism thesis as we examine some applications of *CCD*'s arguments to present-day problems in the international political economy of communication and culture. This chapter's long explanation of a small book (at 126 pages, it would be the shortest he would write) is meant to convey something of the size of the influence *CCD* had at the time it was published. It joined the reading lists with other Schiller works, but it was known worldwide as a contribution of a clear proposal for emancipatory communications within the imperial system. Along with *MCAE* and *The Mind Managers*, this little book helped generate a new discourse within cultural and communication research. Soon after its publication, Schiller also coedited a collection of essays with Kaarle Nordenstreng that provided a comprehensive set of readings to complement the arguments of *CCD*, in particular the importance of national sovereignty as a pivotal point of reflection for discussions of a new order in international communication. This collection, *National Sovereignty and International Communication*, was planned and prepared while Nordenstreng was a visiting professor at UCSD in 1977. The chief university librarian, Melvin J. Voigt, had commissioned the work as the first contribution to the well-known series in information and communication science he started for a small one-person publishing company called Ablex (now part of Greenwood Publishers). The books in this series formed a vital source of critical research in communication throughout the 1970s and into the 1990s. *National Sovereignty and International Communication* was very similar to Schiller and Phillips' *Super-State* in the way it brought together progressive and conservative positions on a key social concept, in this instance to provide an overview of the sovereignty principle, and how it might become a rallying point in the effort to unite an international movement for a new world information order (cf. Kleinwächter 1995, 248).

By now, it goes without saying that Schiller's work sustained a spirited commitment to fundamental social change without being programmatic in tone or purpose. Here again, the political and ethical sensibility rooted in Schiller's experiences in North Africa, postwar Germany, and, we may now add, Allende's Chile in the early 1970s, tempered his thinking about policy discourse as well. Schiller rejected those American functionalist writers who fashioned their arguments around the words "should" and "must" to remind his readers that they are not in the presence of an imperious American who brings solutions for all their problems wrapped up in a nice-looking consultancy report. Still, he knew that policy was about making choices that had tremendous influence over the lives and cultural environment of those affected by it. He had his preferences, of course, but his style of promoting them was much more comradely than commanding, and when he offered his idea of the component parts of an effective policy, he backed up his points with historical rather than functionalist arguments. He suggested that learning from the past is the best way to begin to articulate a forward looking, "non-dominating" policy.

CCD begins with a framing chapter that positions the work as a contribution to the global cultural-communications struggle, which Schiller understood to be taking place both within the United States and internationally. The United States' leadership role in the international political economy had been destabilized by many of the forces discussed previously in *MCAE* and *Mind Managers*, including the Vietnam war; the growing war budget; the movements for civil rights, free speech, and the liberation of women and minorities; and, of course, the Watergate scandal followed by Nixon's and his cabinet's attempts to deceive Congress. Domestic and international communication and cultural struggles accompanied these tensions. On one side, the state-corporate-military alliance was shoring up ever more resources, technologies, and techniques for shaping and managing public consciousness. On the other, a growing number of disenchanted and intrepid media workers were taking up lightweight, affordable communications equipment and developing alternative media sources to shake up prevailing controls over public knowledge.

The political ferment in the postcolonial world also led to many reappraisals of decades of development policy and questions about the role of dominant economic models that had failed to free the two-thirds of the world's population living in abject poverty and dependency. Schiller noted the increasing concern for the cultural components of this dependency, citing national liberation struggles and the Movement of Non-Aligned Nations' efforts to transpose their criticisms of the economic order onto the cultural realm. Many of these criticisms were articulated by the United Nations Conference on Trade and Development (UNCTAD) and UNESCO in the 1960s and early 1970s. He also highlighted a new and important shift in global power with the growth of rival capitalist economies in Japan and Western Europe, which "benefited from strains on the United States economy" (*CCD*, 1–3).

The remaining chapters can be outlined as follows. Chapter 1 presents the structure of cultural domination as the uneven annexation of societies into the "modern world system," using this model as the basis for explaining the history of capitalist expansion worldwide and the West's imperial designs on communication-information.

Chapter 2 critically analyzes the rise and decline of a deceptive promotion of the "free-flow of information" doctrine as a mainstay of U.S. foreign policy (like that in *MCAE*, this was a prescient assessment of the communication component in free-market doctrines that became known in the 1980s and 1990s as neoliberalism). A highly ironic style captures Schiller's view of the hypocrisy of American laissez-faire policy in an historical account of the

United States' attempts to resist communications "free flow" and cultural invasions at a time when the United States was itself a developing and dependent
country.

Chapter 3 argues that after the fortunes of the "free flow" doctrine shifted
in the 1970s, the United States opened another ideological front by promoting
new information technology to strengthen its command over the culture and
communications components of the imperial system. Technology is a social
construct, created to serve dominant users, and applied materially and symboli-
cally to maintain the status quo. Schiller identified the ideological deceptions
of academic promoters of new technologies (such as Daniel Lerner and Ithiel
de Sola Pool) and endorsed the critiques of Garnham and Williams.

Chapter 4 documents the growing dissent among media workers and
national decision-makers in the early 1970s over the media-communications
influence of the United States and how this led to official attempts to formulate
policy around communications and cultural developments. Schiller emphasized the stakes for media workers domestically and internationally as well as
intranational struggles around class, communication/culture, and cultural identity. Schiller described numerous features of a "non-dominating communications system" (*CCD*, 84–97).

In an afterword, Schiller elaborated on the limits of cultural policy with an
assessment of the reforms and counterrevolution in Chilean media during Salvador Allende's government (1971–1973). The Chilean tragedy served as a
poignant example of the difficulties of challenging cultural imperialism
through democratic formulations of policy, but one that nevertheless provoked
Schiller to remain hopeful that increased participation of dominated groups in
the design and operation of a national communications system was still the
"only means of developing and maintaining individual and group consciousness and thus keeping alive the dynamic of change and renewal" (*CCD*, 109;
we return to this point in the conclusion). Such participation fosters conditions
in which "manipulative informational control" cannot thrive, a salutary effect
that Schiller himself seemed to aim for in writing *Communication and Cultural
Domination*. Let's take a closer look at how he did this.

The first thing readers will notice in chapter 1 is Schiller's citation of a scholarly work by Immanuel Wallerstein on the "modern world system." For the
first time, Schiller develops his argument using academic work as a theoretical
point of departure. Though he does not perform an exegesis of Wallerstein's
theory, Schiller does borrow it briefly to frame his discussion of cultural imperialism, finding in "world system" theory a convenient set of terms that help
summarize a number of key points from Schiller's previous work in *MCAE*
and *The Mind Managers*. Basically, the reference to "world system" theory
allowed him to sum up the international relations of power and dependency

that accompanied capitalist modernization, with an emphasis on one of his central concerns: namely, how the organization of the global workforce—the international division of labor—is conditioned by the interaction of capitalism's uneven geographical development with the relative, and changing, positions of dominating and dominated regions over time.

The model identified a geographical core of the system in which the dominant "terms and character of production" that affect all areas operating within reach of the world system are defined. In this model, national states are capable of muddying the " 'pure' workings of the world system," but historical analysis has shown that state interventions have not arrested the system's global expansion. The ensuing expansion created layers of bureaucrats, professionals, experts, and managers. This professional-managerial stratum works to preserve the system in coordination with various national or regional assemblages of dominant interests. An important goal of this group's system-serving work is its own self-preservation (legitimacy), which rests on the public perceiving it as a neutral servant of pluralism and informational transparency. This professional-managerial stratum could also be described as the bureaucratic ensemble, or complexes, that Schiller analyzed in prior work. In short, the "world system" model neatly conveyed Schiller's prior conceptualizations of an institutional "complex" organically tied to the reproduction of the imperial system.

Cultural imperialism fits into the model in a very simple way. Schiller begins with a review of Kaarle Nordenstreng and Tapio Varis' seminal 1974 study showing that communication-information-media mostly flowed in one direction from the core to the periphery of the system (Nordenstreng and Varis 1974). In the "world system" model, the core was defined generally as the West, but when it came to informational flows, Schiller argued that the United States was by far the commanding source of media-related flows from the core to the semiperiphery and periphery of the system. He also acknowledged the growing presence of Western Europe and Japan at the time he wrote (regions that would be considered in the "world system" terminology as semiperipheries ascending to the core). This one-way flow, with its promotion of English as the system's lingua franca, "represents the reality of power" (*CCD*, 6).

Moreover, in addition to the dominant sources and languages, the technical base supporting system maintenance and enabling the unidirectional flow of information-culture-communication "is sought, discovered, and developed" by the dominant class at the system's core. On this point, as we have seen, Schiller was well prepared to offer a detailed history of broadcast, satellite, and cable communications to show how technology has been intentionally shaped to serve the status quo first, while any liberatory or life-enhancing features have either been accidental or afterthoughts provoked by social protest. He summarized his earlier research on this matter, but before doing so he inserted an important note of caution against an instrumentalist view of technology: "These instruments," he said, "could, at a later time, provide a basis for the transformation that would replace the prevailing structure," even though they "presently serve and enhance the system of domination" (*CCD*, 6).

In another important passage defining cultural imperialism, Schiller added an additional caution against economic determinism. The passage was also significant because it was the first explicitly polemical statement he had made in any of his writings about another international communications researcher. Schiller took issue with William Read's argument that recognizing the economic basis of commercial media expansion was sufficient to show that cultures were affected by "America's mass media mercantilists." Schiller not only questioned why Read would use an anachronism such as mercantilism to describe imperialism, but, more importantly, he showed that while the economic imperative was an important cause of cultural penetration, it was not preeminent in the consequences that followed.

To explain this point, Schiller described cultural and economic forces working interdependently whenever U.S. or European multinational communications and media firms located operations in weaker countries. They not only proffered messages from the core but also brought a number of sociological influences that altered the way "all socializing institutions of the affected host area" functioned (*CCD*, 8–9). His first examples included the dominant language of the penetrating business (English), the imported organizational models, and the mode of communication within and between the large firms. This "business culture" demanded a certain amount of synchronization of all participating local organizations, thus spreading a way of doing things, the relations of production, from the core to the periphery. This was a sociological proposition about the way "institutional networks" form on the ground and grow, absorbing regions and nations into the larger system. Again, this could easily be worded as a relation between the exported core communications complex and the imperial system. What was clear was that the world capitalist economy outfitted its complexes with "its production, its working force, its rewards, its investments, and its resource priorities." The subsidiary branches of the core communications-information complex therefore served as more than agents of a profit-seeking, competitive media firm. They were also cultural agents whose presence changed the very "infrastructure of socialization" (*CCD*, 9).

Having set out these cautions against instrumentalism and economic determinism, Schiller states what has become one of the most widely quoted definitions of cultural imperialism:

In this sense, the concept of cultural imperialism today best describes the sum of processes by which a society is brought into the modern world system and how its dominating stratum is attracted, pressured, forced, and sometimes bribed into shaping social institutions to correspond to, or even promote, the values and structures of the dominating center of the system. (*CCD*, 9)

His second set of examples illustrating the workings of cultural imperialism would be very familiar to readers of his previous works. They focused more on the cultural curricula produced in academia and by the media. The content of broadcasting and film, for example, changes with the adoption of commercial market criteria, whether advertising-based or, as in the case of film, modeled on Hollywood fare rather than on national or local culture. On the question of indigenous culture, Schiller briefly described the phenomenon of localized versions of global media and how Disney, for instance, marketed its cartoon characters to mirror local traditions of language and costume in a barely disguised effort to hide content aimed at producing positive associations with the capitalist world system directed by a benign American leadership.

From the brief textual example of media content Schiller moved again to examples of sociological effects. He showed how the export of American-style business culture and communications occurred through an apparent "educational philanthropy" when U.S. universities as well as the Agency for International Development (AID) created programs in peripheral nations. Teaching the "American business ethos" or American-style journalism to next-generation managers and media-makers was not only about the transfer of skills. It also encouraged the adoption of foreign work routines and dispositions toward the creative process that were divorced from local tradition, easing the way for the acceptance of a corporate-commercial interpretation of the value of life. Other examples from this set focused on the relations of production—that is, the organization of human interaction and routines—as they were imposed via subsidiaries of multinational corporations. Linked to this is the way scientific-technical research and development (R&D) has historically been designed to serve the priorities of these powerful corporations, along with military and state bureaucratic needs. Financial support defined what was worthy science, resulting in further synchronization of national interests and market criteria.

These last examples underscore an important feature of Schiller's cultural imperialism theory: The command over the international division of informational labor is a fundamental necessity for the dominating core of the system. The process involves the replication throughout the periphery of the class structure of the core countries. As such, socialist thinking would be discouraged, and socialist policies and leaderships would not be tolerated.

In *MCAE*, Schiller showed how the U.S. government and military developed communications systems to support the containment or destruction of socialist projects around the world. Here, he added the tourist industry, commercialized sports, and Westernized media organizations to talk about how a positive association with the capitalist system can be nurtured by the presence of culture industries in countries that are still considering socialist or socialist-leaning policies. As Schiller pointed out, the economic incentives offered through these culture industries were very often irresistible to the ruling groups in the semiperiphery and periphery. And here, again, *CCD* marked a significant addition to Schiller's previous work on the cultural components of imperialism. Recognition of the consent, solicitation, and efforts of national leadership in the periphery to incorporate their societies into the world system led Schiller to think it had become "inappropriate to describe the contemporary mechanics of cultural control as the outcome of 'invasion,' though I, too, have used this term in the past" (*CCD*, 16).

This was a crucial modification of Schiller's earlier understanding of cultural imperialism as it was articulated in *MCAE* and *The Mind Managers*. *CCD* was unique for including the component of a national leadership's class identification in its analysis, which wasn't true of most accounts of cultural imperialism. We can imagine that this analysis of internal national power structures was provoked by his growing collaboration with writers and critics in the Third World, the rising number of struggles of national liberation, even endeavors to disassociate from the world system, of which he was an acute observer, and by his study of the issues and problems at the center of the emerging research and debates on national communications policy.

This key point in Schiller's work also helped it to stand out to many Third World readers as a realistic appraisal of the conditions in which national policy would be formulated. This was the case of Manjunath Pendakur, who would become a leading voice of anti-imperialism within the community of international communication scholars. Pendakur was taken by Schiller's clear recognition of the role played by a national ruling class dependent on foreign capital for its existence, which Pendakur called in his important study of the Canadian film industry the "comprador bourgeoisie." After leaving his job as a camera operator for a CBS affiliate in Seattle in the mid 1970s, Pendakur went to study with Dallas Smythe (whose work he had chanced upon while browsing in a Seattle library) at Simon Fraser University, where he read both *MCAE* and *CCD*. Pendakur recalled that when "Reading Schiller's work and, particularly his theory of cultural imperialism, I felt empowered" (interview July 23, 2002). Schiller warned of national elites in the newly independent countries who might use the language of cultural resistance in self-serving ways to reinstate oppressive, self-advancing cultural institutions. This was precisely the political reality that Pendakur came to know growing up in India after the British colonialists departed. For "those of us who were coming out of the colonial experience, Herb's words were not mere words; they resonated with great meaning" about the postcolonial condition (Pendakur 2001, 44).

While Schiller took seriously the "collaborative role of the ruling groups in the dominated areas of the world capitalist economy," he nevertheless argued that primary responsibility for the one-way flow rested with the "initiating drives from the center of the system" (*CCD*, 17). Schiller insisted that the United States and, to a lesser but growing extent, Western European and Japanese conglomerates held tremendous power to define criteria for determining resource allocation, what was made, how it was made, and where it was made. Monetary, political, and military power helped to ensure matters in the world system were as the core demanded they be, and, in the process, shaped and structured "consciousness throughout the system at large" (*CCD*, 17).

The chapter on cultural imperialism ends with a reminder that the system, however powerful it has become, was still unstable at its core. From worldwide economic depressions, to world war, to the war in Vietnam—the system has shown a tendency toward crisis and waste. The political leadership of the United States and throughout the world had been challenged by the organized efforts of students and workers in many nations. The strain on the government's legitimacy and ability to rule was exacerbated in the United States by scandal and the inflationary spiral of the 1970s. The West could not seriously present itself as a model of progress and unending prosperity, and doubts were even expressed by leading groups within the core. As resistance to imperialism rose around the world during the 1960s, the U.S. military and corporate leadership rushed to bring communication satellites into the service of "crisis management" and generated study after study of the importance of communications media in promoting foreign policy. This was the substance of Schiller's previous research for *MCAE* and *The Mind Managers*.

When cultural domination and pro-system consciousness cannot be guaranteed by simple economic means, control over the "informational apparatus" becomes even more important to the ruling groups. How the media and culture work, how influence is produced, what audiences think—these become questions the core leadership must have answers for. Enter international communications research in the service of American imperial aspirations. Schiller cited a study by his friend and IAMCR colleague Hamid Mowlana that counted and coded research related to international communication published between 1850 and 1970. It showed the research spiked between 1960 and 1969, when more than half of all international communications research was produced. What was the focus of this research, according to Mowlana? "Studies in specific cultural and geographical areas have corresponded roughly to United States involvement in those areas" (quoted in *CCD*, 20). Allied with this research was a new area of mind management called "public diplomacy"

aimed at using communication research and work in related professional fields
to get "a grip on the minds of foreign audiences so that the foreign policies of
the United States or, for that matter, any nation utilizing such techniques are
admired, or at least accepted and tolerated" (*CCD*, 20). Finally, most of the
research Schiller referred to was based on audience polling and social and psychological modeling of audience behavior for predictive purposes. Schiller
included the work of the United States Information Agency (USIA) in this
group of imperial communications research units. All could be linked to the
influence of advertising and public relations in shaping public knowledge and
political communication, which has continued to grow since Schiller first analyzed it in *The Mind Managers*.

As mentioned above, chapter 2 of *CCD* treated the academic and government discourse of "the free flow of information" with irony and scorn. The
doctrine was only promoted by the U.S. leadership after the United States had
secured its position as the sole world capitalist power. Before then, the United
States recognized that British communication dominance, and incidentally
British promotion of a "free flow" policy, was to be resisted via a mixture of
protectionist policies and commercial initiatives to gain control of international
wire communication and publishing. Consider in this context that the founding of RCA, the Radio Corporation of America, in 1920 was based on expro-
priation of a British firm (American Marconi), an alliance of U.S. military and
monopoly capitalist enterprises holding key patents to wireless radio, and a
commercial effort to capture the market for international communications
away from the British (Barnouw 1966). This episode set the stage for subsequent lobbying attempts by the U.S. commercial press, an ascendant power in
the international news market before World War II, to get the doctrine of a
free press and "free flow of information" on the national policy agenda. By
war's end, the free flow doctrine was moved from national policy to the center
of U.S. foreign policy when the United States was the lone hegemon in the
world system.

By the end of the 1940s, the United States had convinced its Western part-
ners to accept "free flow" and "made certain that the newly created United
Nations, and the related United Nations Educational, Cultural, and Scientific
Organization (UNESCO), would put great emphasis on the free flow issue."
In fact, the founding proposals for UNESCO already contained "free flow" as
a basic principle in 1945 (*CCD*, 33). Schiller reminded readers that in the
immediate postwar period the United States held a preeminent position of
influence in both the UN and UNESCO, where it could exercise an "auto-
matic majority" whenever it desired a vote be taken on an issue affecting it.
European member states were dependent on the United States for aid, Latin
American members bent under the hemispheric weight of U.S. military and

economic power, and the remaining members from the Middle East, Africa, and Asia were still subject to "the Western empire system" (CCD, 32). The United States used UNESCO's embrace of "free flow" as an important "semantic strategy" for the hard sell of U.S. foreign policy and commercial media interests to friend and foe alike. Resistance to the idea, in particular from countries with state or public ownership of the media, was treated by American proponents as a rejection of the "ethical imperative" of freedom itself (CCD, 29–30). The United States' leadership even dismissed as "a justification for censorship" recommendations from a panel of American culture and arts experts that the content of this "free flow" should possess qualities that provide "positive and creative service to the cause of international understanding and therefore peace" (CCD, 34–35).

The result of this exercise in power politics was an international trading environment, based on the "free flow" doctrine, that ensured an onslaught of American-made media exports and a surge in the importance of foreign markets to American cultural industries. Interest in international audiences as a subject of communications research accompanied this growth, as did a remarkable increase in the use of opinion poll and consumer survey research to track the tastes and habits of consumers of U.S. media as well as the manufactured goods that flowed with the growing presence of advertising everywhere (a sector then dominated by U.S. firms).

The nature of all these institutions of cultural imperialism was covered in depth in *The Mind Managers*. What set *CCD* apart was Schiller's analysis of the cracks that appeared in the consensus over the "free flow" doctrine in the 1970s. The United States' strong-arm tactics forcing "free flow" on national governments was not forgotten, and by the late 1960s, notions of "cultural sovereignty, cultural privacy, cultural autonomy, and even admissions of the possibility of cultural imperialism" were already circulating in international forums and writings (CCD, 39). Of course, these weren't the first quarrels with the "free flow" idea. Schiller recalled early warnings in the 1948 Hutchins Commission report on freedom of the press, which pointed out the inherent contradiction in the "free flow" principle—that conditions increasing information quantity cannot exist, as the "free flow" doctrine held, without also creating particular kinds of information with social and cultural consequences (the question of informational quality). The Hutchins Commission's concerns were borne out in the late 1960s, when an alarming list of consequences was beginning to appear on policy agendas of many countries. By the early to mid 1970s, even UNESCO was veering away from its support of the doctrine (CCD, 39–40).

Efforts within UNESCO to urge the United States to accept international cooperation, in particular where new satellite technology was concerned, met with an incredible reaction from the U.S. leadership, which saw "the right of nations to control the character of the messages transmitted into their territories both dangerous and a gross violation of the U.S. Constitution's provision concerning freedom of speech" (*CCD*, 41). This view equated corporate rights with individual rights and infringements on commerce with infringements on free speech. In his book *Culture Inc.* (1989), Schiller would deconstruct this discourse and the legal decisions that disguised it as natural law. For now, he was merely stunned, but not totally surprised, by the hubris of the United States' ruling groups who denounced international cooperation as an act of prior censorship.

Freedom of information is a wonderful idea in principle, but Schiller saw how in practice it could be used to exploit existing relations of power. In Schiller's words:

> When there is an uneven distribution of power among individuals or groups *within* nations or *among* nations, a free hand—freedom to continue doing what led to the existing condition—serves to strengthen the already powerful and weaken further the already frail. Evidence of this abounds in all aspects of modern life—in race, sex, and occupational and international relationships. Freedoms that are formally impressive may be substantively oppressive when they reinforce prevailing inequalities while claiming to be providing generalized opportunity for all. (*CCD, 45*)

By 1975, leading figures in the United States' communications-military-corporate enterprises were worried that, as Frank Stanton (former head of CBS) put it, "the capacity of America to dictate the course of international events has diminished" (quoted in *CCD*, 22). Their preeminence had relied on "the free flow of information," which was intertwined with the "imperial ascendancy of the United States." The "free flow" doctrine was fading (we should note, only temporarily) as the U.S. leadership sought an alternative policy discourse to maintain its advantage over rival economies and rival political positions emerging in newly formulated national communications policy. Technology proved to be an adequate alternative, and the United States used its massive R&D capabilities and manufacturing plant to rush new communications technologies into an international situation in which its hegemony was at stake. The technology in question was a combination of telecommunication satellites and computers. This technology of cultural domination is the subject of *CCD's* chapter 3.

Briefly, Schiller described a number of plans and proposals for the new global networks that the leading figures in the United States offered to the international community. Among these was an as-yet-undeveloped wave of interconnected, high-speed, broadband networks for international electronic mail and data transmission. All the technology discussed was by nature transnational, and immediately obviated the role of national political safeguards that were then being contemplated by many nations in the periphery and semiperiphery of the world system. Schiller suggested that this battle would play out in unknown ways, but that certain features of technology should be understood before policy-makers, especially in the informational "have not" countries, too quickly succumbed to the seductions of satellite and computer technologies. As we see in the following chapter, Schiller intensified his research on information technology and markets in the 1970s in order to thicken this critique of the so-called information society. While the basis of this critique was laid out in *MCAE* and *The Mind Managers*, Schiller's argument became more incisive in *CCD*. It can be summarized as follows.

Advanced communication and information technologies are material channels through which dominating forms of culture and communication can flow, but they are also and at the same time symbolic expressions of the dominating culture. Schiller broadly construed technology to include not just the machinery but also the techniques associated with routines and operative dispositions in large, modern economic complexes. These prevailing routines, or relations of production, condition the development of technology, while the technology in turn functions to duplicate those relations and ensure their fixity in social institutions. Hence, each technological advance, planned for system-serving innovation, was proscribed in a way that embedded solutions, not for general social problems, but for maintaining the already fixed social relations and commanding position of the dominating center over the division of labor. Of course, mistakes can happen and the process can be disrupted, but this was the dominant pattern. The concept of a new international division of labor (NIDL) became central to the pattern Schiller perceived here, and while his thinking on the NIDL emerges fully in subsequent works, Schiller's effort in *CCD* to understand the consequences of reorganizing labor on a global scale raised important questions even at this early stage in his research on new technology applications.

This approach to technology informed Schiller's critique of the "developmentalist" paradigm in international communications. He argued that Lerner and others, in particular the group at the Massachusetts Institute of Technology, which included Ithiel de Sola Pool, got the sequence of development backward—the technology was sought, "discovered," and advanced by core countries only after they had achieved a certain level of industrial development. They in turn made these technologies available in poor sections of the world, their design intact with a priori aims. Moreover, said Schiller, the proposition that mass communication technology was a key to modernization was based on a false claim—there had been neither historical precedents nor sociological evidence showing that an unindustrialized country had ever leapt to an advanced economic stage on the basis of communication technology alone.

> The process that Western academics call "modernization" generally follows the intro-duction of the business system, its commercial arrangements, financial networks, eco-nomic activities, and not least, its technological structures and processes. It is all of these, *in toto*, that initiate and *require* the modernization campaigns. And it is the tech-nology—broadly defined as organizational structures, administrative hierarchies, and, of course, equipment and processes—that determines the fundamental communica-tions patterns. (*CCD*, 49)

The appearance of technology as mere equipment, gadgetry, circuitry, and so on hides these social origins and gives the impression that these are just inan-imate pieces of hardware whose essential neutrality makes them employable under any sociopolitical arrangements. Schiller provided several examples to show the concrete purposes of technology planned via government-military-corporate research and development. Here, he drew on the critical writings of Garnham, Williams, and Smythe to further refine his argument that "technol-ogy is a social construct and serves the prevailing system of social power, though it often contributes to changes in the organization and distribution of that power" (*CCD*, 51). Schiller argued that the failures of advanced technol-ogy to live up to the promises of futurists and propagandists were best under-stood in light of the tremendous strains on the environment caused by military-industrial designs and the "the quest for profitability" (*CCD*, 53). Of course, one had to be aware of the environmental strains in order to perceive these failures. Alas, as Schiller pointed out, public knowledge about the environ-mental damage caused by Western technology has been distorted by the "sys-tem-serving informational apparatus" that has persisted in depicting pollution, rising cancer rates, and growing evidence of physical and psychological harms as mysterious but inescapable side effects of modern life. Further distorting this reality, dominant informational channels (all high technology businesses) have promoted modern technology as the remedy (rather than cause) of environ-mental ills.

The tone of disbelief in Schiller's writing culminated with a call to find an alternative to the technological solution for the problems faced by countries now considering national communications policy, in particular where those policies contemplated the use of satellite-based telecommunications and com-puter networks. Schiller asked finally, "Is an alternative conceivable?" (*CCD*, 55). He answered by recalling that the course of technological development historically has been determined by a collective process in which the distribu-tion of social influence and authority were paramount. To make his point, he cited a study by Nicholas Garnham on the efforts of the Luddite movement.

In early-nineteenth-century England, weavers calling themselves "Ned Ludd's Army" attacked workshops employing factory-style production. They named themselves after the imaginary folk hero, Ned Ludd, whose resistance to brutal technology had been memorialized in folk tales. The Luddites opposed the introduction of new weaving machines and industrial techniques of production. The reasons they did this have been historically maligned and "deliberately misinterpreted" by generations of anti-Luddite intellectuals and political pundits. In actuality, the Luddites wanted new technology to help relieve backstraining work; what they didn't want was to lose control over the work process by allowing the proposed new technology and factory techniques to centralize control in the hands of factory managers. Their exclusion from the planning process ensured that the technology would be employed to further their exploitation, not to enhance their working conditions.

For Schiller, then, the first step in planning alternative technologies was ensuring *participation of all affected sectors* of the society in the planning process. At the time he wrote this, only 1 percent of all R&D investment in the world was directed to solving problems in developing countries. That situation had to be addressed to meet the needs represented in the R&D planning processes. After participation, the next step was to guarantee a level of *self-reliance*. This position was the only reasonable response to the voluminous evidence of West-

Herbert Schiller, University of California at San Diego, 1978.

ern technology's failures and social costs. Self-reliance could help ensure that any technological transfers were done on the basis of *selective association* with the core countries. John Lent's work in Malaysia demonstrated for Schiller how the United States not only exported the technology, color TV sets in this case, but how it also exported a kind of social frenzy with the technology—a frenzy based on a threatening feeling that nonadoption of the latest industrial wonder would leave people in the dark ages. This frenzy to buy the latest version of a particular gadget was well understood in the hyperconsumerist United States, but did this anxiety have to be spread to the rest of the world?

Schiller suggested that self-reliance and selectivity were prerequisites for the *deceleration* of transfers of technology and other accouterments of Western developmentalism. Steps taken for such deliberation, caution, abstention, restraint, and deceleration were necessary for an alternative planning process. Schiller added more evidence for this: The quick uptake of biotechnology crippled a number of agricultural economies in the periphery where their sustainable crop production, dependent on crop rotation and diversity, was transformed to high-yield, single crop production based on a frenetic effort, imposed in some cases by monetary pressures of the World Bank and IMF, to adopt the United States' agricultural techniques and technology.

Schiller turned to a fuller assessment in chapter 4 of the national communications policies emerging in the early 1970s. He framed this phenomenon as "class conflict" moving on a global scale "into the communications-cultural sphere in an *explicit* way; and the emergence of national communications policies [as] the reflection of generally still-unresolved battles between contradictory interests and demands in the cultural-informational sector" (*CCD*, 68). Class and nation merged in this movement to articulate culture-communication and policy. For many in the postwar generation of leftist internationalists, the cause of national liberation was a manifestation of the political realignment of the ideologies of nation, socialism, and the international labor movement that accompanied the defeat of fascism. There was great hope that this was the renewal of socialist opposition within a distinctly national cultural framework. The adoption of socialist ideas in the postcolonial struggles of national liberation also reflected this elision of class and national interests to oppose the postwar imperialism of the United States, drawing in particular from writings of Lenin and Stalin on national self-determination and socialist revolution (for more on this ideological realignment, see Hobsbawm 1992).

In the context of this historical movement, Schiller understood the push for a nationally oriented policy to defend national cultural identity not only as an effort of dominated classes in many nations to resist an imperious American cultural presence, but also as an expression of resistance to the further entrenchment of the capitalist class system on a global scale. This struggle could be seen throughout the system. In the core, more control over the course of national communication policy became a vital concern for the state-capital team in their "common front" against labor and the general improvement of the informational resources available during nonwork time. Leaders in the industrialized world were attempting to install greater ideological control via national policies to shore up loyalty within the system's core, which had suffered widespread worker and student resistance to government policy in the 1960s and 1970s. During this same period, a growing portion of the working class in the core and semiperiphery were winning shorter work hours, causing businesses to increase the flow of commercial messages to help transform "free" time into consumption time.

Schiller saw another possible, and closely related, line of debate in the national communications policy arena having to do with industrial conditions of the labor force most closely associated with the production of the messages and meanings. Here he only briefly remarked on the dislocation of workers caused on one hand by the concentration of capital in the communications-entertainment industries and on the other by the technology and techniques that reduced the labor contribution. If social participation in policy-making efforts ended up including such workers, which Schiller tended to doubt, then the demands of adversely affected workers may well bring another important contribution to the policy debates.

In addition to the globalization of class struggle via national communications policy, Schiller also saw intercapitalist and interstate rivalries as significant conflicts emerging in the widening battle over the direction and control of national communications. When influential national and multinational corporations participated in policy debates, they assured that issues such as trade, tariffs, subsidies, and other matters that could make or break a dominant market position would be inscribed into the discourse of national communication-cultural policy. The demand for some form of protection from U.S. multinational firms could also easily be couched in national culturalist terms to the benefit of the national industries and investors who tried to influence policy. While these were generally private commercial firms, larger public utilities also made a powerful impact on national policy protections. They were largely involved in interstate rivalries over the strategic position of national industries in the international market.

These interstate rivalries were often motivated by U.S. allies' lingering resentment of the "free flow" doctrine, which subordinated their national media and communications operations to U.S. market domination. These disputes did much to foster the policy discourse of national cultural sovereignty and cultural self-defense against U.S. cultural imperialism in the 1970s. By 1973, Canada and many West European countries had initiated new national policy discussions; a year earlier Finland and UNESCO generated new policy ideas for national communications media. By 1975, the British Labour Party, Peruvian Military Government, Colombia, and the Movement of Non-Aligned Nations had all issued policy statements that in some way suggested the need to develop and defend a national communications system against the expansion of American cultural imperialism.

To further clarify his approach to the national communication policy debate, Schiller contrasted his analysis with one of the leading lights of the dominant paradigm of international communications, Ithiel de Sola Pool, who was also writing at the same time about the proliferation of the policy-making initiatives. Pool's conclusions diverged radically from Schiller's, not to mention that he ridiculed the assessment of nearly 130 countries whose representatives had called for change in the global communication system. Pool argued that there was no empirical need for national policies. He suggested instead that more efficiency was needed in the system itself, which would be provided by expert technical consultants. Policy invited too much participation for Pool, where archaic notions like sovereignty or social needs could muck up real research into the technical details of system efficiency. Schiller cited this argument as evidence of what can be expected from the intellectual sector at the core of the system. His critique centered on Pool's portrayal of communication policy research as a neutral instrument, a position that Schiller argued was a disguise for the ideological framework in which the research operated. Pool promoted social scientific facts as the only trustworthy source for solving international communication inefficiencies. Schiller concluded that Pool's condescending caricature of nonexperts as pontificating "pseudo-philosophers" was merely a shameless attempt to disavow the political-ethical problems at the heart of the system Pool defended (quoted in *CCD*, 83–84).

Schiller went further. He argued that Pool's denial of the empirical need for rethinking national communication policy was an attempt to deflect scrutiny from the de facto policy that already existed in the most advanced market economy. Pool's claim that communication media operate best on the basis of technical and economic efficiency alone was the same claim made by the for-profit media sector in the United States. That there is no "prescribed set of rules and codes" did not, however, mean that institutionalized forms of behavior, values, and routines were absent from the national communications systems. Schiller called this hidden set of policies "institutionalized communication domination." Schiller conceived of this form of domination as analogous to institutionalized racism or sexism, which are unstated policies of white male privilege that organize and sustain hierarchies within social organizations. These fixed hierarchies bar nonwhites and women from the salary structures, professions, and positions of influence that are accorded to white men by virtue of their skin color and sex. Likewise, institutionalized communication domination is the unstated policy that guarantees that large commercial communications facilities are defined as superior (to educational, noncommercial, and other organizations) by virtue of their income-generating properties, despite their nondemocratic character, their primary function as advertising channels, and their standards of efficiency and value—which are determined by private owner and investor satisfaction, not by social considerations. Consider also the fact that the U.S. government has never had a department at the administrative level devoted to cultural policy, frustrating attempts by other nations with established ministries or departments of culture to locate a peer U.S. entity with which to negotiate international relations regarding media, communication, and culture. The absence of such an entity has both obscured the operations of the United States' de facto cultural-communication policy and made international treaties virtually impossible to reach.

Schiller argued for policy-making that would dismantle the foundation of these institutional forms of domination. Until such a fundamental challenge was mounted, Schiller feared that the tacit policy would continue to work unnoticed, except by weaker groups adversely affected by it. Just as the civil rights movement and the women's movement brought the concerns of oppressed groups into conflict with the established order to initiate debates for equality in all social institutions (ongoing in the United States), Schiller saw demands to overturn the dominating communications apparatus arising out of conditions of conflict between the dominating core and a dominated periphery. The U.S. leadership, with support of academic boosters such as Pool, reacted against these demands by pressing harder for the nonpolicy-sounding policy of "free flow." (In this context, it is interesting to consider how a similar kind of semantic strategy has used "color-blind, gender-blind" policy positions to defend white, male privilege against demands for positive discrimination or affirmative action.)

So what were the features of a "nondominating" communication policy envisioned in *CCD*? Because Schiller's contribution can still become a vital part of our own work of critical communications in the twenty-first century, that question is addressed in more detail in the concluding chapter. For now, it is important to again underscore Schiller's view that the creation of a nondominating policy begins by identifying and understanding the conflict between the weak and strong, the haves and the have-nots. Schiller saw this conflict in general terms as an inherent problem for the system and continued to view the struggle between haves and have-nots as an essential component in his approach to cultural imperialism. He never forgot the lessons of his youth, which continued to guide his thinking on the basic questions of international communication research and policy analysis. Perhaps this is why throughout

CCD Schiller asks readers to beware the intellectual studies that claim to provide neutral, expert assessments of technological needs in the not-yet industrialized periphery. Such assessment "has been traditionally undertaken by the same groups and interests that control the research and the products that research stimulates" (*CCD*, 64). We should remember when reading the positive endorsements of new information technologies (telematics or the combinations of satellite, cable, and computerized telecommunication networks) that they have given transnational forces the ability to bypass political safeguards that were necessary for making independent national communications policy in the have-not countries. Schiller also began to recognize in this period of his writing that telematics made feasible a new global scale of labor exploitation and control demanded by the transnational enterprises.

For Schiller, the internationalization of the class system was a fundamental reality that had largely eluded the debates in UNESCO and elsewhere where national policies were contemplated. For the most part, discussions of national policy in the 1970s and 1980s disavowed the reality of class that Schiller and only a handful of others in the field of international communication had addressed (Gerald Sussman, Manjunath Pendakur, John Lent, Janet Wasko, and Vincent Mosco, among others). The result of this absence shifted the weight of cultural policy debate entirely to questions of national cultural identity. Schiller did not foresee this shift when he wrote *CCD*, but the result was a prevailing view of cultural imperialism that encouraged critical communication theorists to champion often oppressive traditionalism and ruling national elites in the name of defending cultural identity (see Miller et al. 2001, 17–43 and passim).

In the years after *CCD* was published, Schiller began to modify his theory of cultural imperialism to account for empirical changes in the international class system. By the time he was completing *CCD* and carrying out the research for his next book, he began to take notice of early signs of the American economy's changing position in the world system and the rising importance of transnational corporate complexes. In this reconfigured world system, more than half of the hundred biggest economies would come to be controlled not by nation-states, but by transnational corporations, four hundred of which would eventually account for two-thirds of the world's fixed assets and 70 percent of world trade already concentrated in North America, Western Europe, and Japan (Miller et al. 2001, 39–40). But as Schiller studied how these transnational amalgamations extended to the main levers and sites of economic activity in the cultural sphere, Schiller concluded that "American cultural imperialism is not dead." Rather, the older form of cultural imperialism "no longer adequately describes the global cultural condition. Today it is more useful to view transnational corporate culture as the central force, with a continuing heavy flavor of U.S. media know-how, derived from long experience with marketing and entertainment skills and practices" (*MCAE* 1992, 14–15).

Cultural imperialism may not be "American" in the way it once was, thanks to the rise of the transnational corporation as a powerful economic agent, and to the acquiescence of most countries to the economic policy of "free flow" and the class system it supports (this arrangement is known as the Washington Consensus—the *tout ensemble* of corporate freedom, boundary-less capital, the marketplace, and government involvement only as enforcer of market economics). As we see in the next chapter, many Third World leaders were drawn into this class system by the seductions of information technology and American aid. Of course, U.S. military invasion or the mere threat of invasion served as another strong inducement to join the system. Schiller put it this way: "No nation endeavoring to create an alternative social order was left alone by the military. Threats of armed force created impossible conditions for whatever limited social experimentation was attempted" (*MCAE* 1992, 21).

The first years of the twenty-first century began with worldwide economic and political crises, the road to renewal uncertain. In a previous crisis economy, the United States promoted information technology as the source of economic revival throughout the world system. The following chapter focuses on this strategic effort and the rivalries within the world system over who would lead the new "information economy."

Chapter Five

Deceptions and Contradictions of the "Information Age"

What forces other nations to board the electronics bandwagon is no simple desire for human improvement. It originates with the competitive drives of the world business system. It comes from the fear of being excluded from markets, losing employment, and being forced further down the economic ladder into deeper dependence. The deluge of new information equipment, processes, and products created by the staggering military outlays in the U.S. whips the world community into the game of follow-the-leader, regardless of need or utility.

—Herbert Schiller, *Information and the Crisis Economy*, 23

As we have seen in preceding chapters, Schiller understood informational resources, information technology, and informational labor as sites of conflict within the world system. The struggles of affected countries in the periphery to ensure equitable relations—economic, political, and cultural-informational—between dominating and dominated regions met with a range of responses from the leadership in advanced industrialized countries, from complacent indifference and paternalist scolding to economic extortion and armed intervention. The United States led the reactionary team against the struggling countries, developing and using advanced information and communication technology to help them contain an "insurgent world," as Schiller put it in *Information and the Crisis Economy* (1984). At the same time, the United States sought to defend its hegemony against all rivals, rich and poor, via "barriers down" diplomacy and a doctrinaire position that asserted that volumes of free-flowing information, with no mention of content or quality, was the sufficient and necessary condition for uninterrupted profit-making and an unyielding campaign against Soviet socialism. Political dissent in the United States was met with further corporate-military-government encroachments on the infra-

85

structures of socialization and consciousness-shaping. Interstate rivalries among advanced industrial countries and intercapitalist conflicts among media and communications enterprises generated additional demands for strategic information technology and operating materials, but also amplified the calls for international agreements and policies to bring order to core communications arrangements. The state-capital rivalries did, however, share one "common front"—that is, to force upon the global workforce the burden of whatever arrangements emerged from these adjustments to the international communications complex.

These social conflicts have been discussed in some detail in previous chapters; their description and analysis were at the center of Schiller's procedural aim of shattering the media-made myth that social conflict does not exist. These historically specific conflicts and contradictions comprised for Schiller the general features of the cultural-informational condition at the time when the ballyhoo about the new information age began. This chapter examines

Herbert Schiller, University of Stockholm, 1978.

Schiller's turn to the analysis of that new age. But before we start, it is important for readers to pause to imagine (or remember) a time without answering machines, modems, the Internet, the World Wide Web, desktop computers, digital television, caller ID, cell phones, product scanners in supermarkets, "smart" cards, computerized card catalogues, and any number of the "everyday" artifacts and appliances that permeate our lives in advanced industrialized-informationalized-computerized countries. That time is where we begin.

There are three identifiable stages of development in this period of Schiller's research and writing. They responded to a decade that Cees Hamelink described as "years of accommodation and deceptive international consensus [when] thinking had to be devoted to expose the power games in the world arena that obscured the real issues and that were aimed to mislead the less powerful players" (2001, 11). Schiller's first contribution to that task was represented by the book *Who Knows: Information in the Age of the Fortune 500*, published in 1981. The second involved the work of refining the research initiated with *Who Knows*. This effort culminated in the book *Information and the Crisis Economy* (hereafter *ICE*), published in 1984. In purpose and style, *ICE* recalls *Communication and Cultural Domination*, the formal similarity of the titles effectively mirroring parallel concerns and continuities through almost a decade of work. Like *Communication and Cultural Domination*, *ICE* is a work of synthesis and political analysis aimed at contributing to a wider debate over information and cultural policy. *ICE* also introduced two subjects that formed a bridge to the third stage in Schiller's thinking and writing in this period. One was the growing atmosphere of political-informational repression in the United States and the other involved his intervention into intellectual debates over the relation of political economy to culture. Both of these subjects stand out in the third major work of the 1980s, *Culture Inc: The Corporate Takeover of Public Expression*, published in 1989. As we see in the next chapter, *Culture Inc.* is a repudiation of the institutions and discourses that engendered much of the suffocating political and cultural conditions of late-twentieth-century America.

This chapter considers the first two works, *Who Knows: Information in the Age of the Fortune 500* and *ICE*, as a single strand of progress in Schiller's thinking and writing. Again, my intention is to highlight what I think are the significant advances in Schiller's work and how that work contributed to critical communications scholarship. There will be an opportunity to consider how we might apply the analysis to the present period, more of which is taken up in the concluding chapter, and also what we might modify to account for empirical changes that have occurred since the 1980s when Schiller wrote these books. Absent in this chapter is the examination of methods and sourcing, which have remained relatively stable in all of his works. However, there are two exceptions in this period of writing worth noting. One was that Schiller increasingly drew, for various purposes of his argument, on a growing body of critical communications and cultural analysis and commentary. The other was an effect of the processes under study: The privatization of information, especially government agency reports, increased the frequency with which researchers such as Schiller—that is, those with no major funding or relation to the power centers—encountered barriers of access to important documentation that was publicly funded and produced for the top crust of decision-making groups. The diminished ability to "listen in" on the dominating sectors was not just a matter of making adjustments to his method, however frustrating those were for Schiller as a researcher. Such difficulties were also treated in *Who Knows* as examples of enclosures around information vital to a deliberative democratic order. The privatization of vital social information marks out one of the main themes: This is a book about who knows, not necessarily about what they know, because that information is being commoditized, privatized, and secreted away as a form of property by major (Fortune 500) corporations.

The historical conditions that motivated Schiller's ten-year burst of intellectual activity in the 1980s, remarkably more vigorous as he neared his seventieth birthday, can be summarized as follows. In the 1970s, pundits, politicians, and academics in the advanced industrialized countries were entranced by thoughts of an electronic chrome-plated wonderland, built on computerized technologies and networks, that would herald the next evolutionary stage of unending prosperity in the capitalist market system. The media said so, professors were saying so, management gurus concurred, and the U.S. leadership was telling the American people it was so. For Schiller, these were not merely efforts of mind management but represented what he called "a pincers movement against the public's knowledgeability" (*Who Knows*, 74) about what was actually going on, which was, as he reported in *Who Knows*, a fundamental restructuring of the international economy.

In the 1980s, with economic stagnation threatening the world system, the earlier hype was toned down into a more somber, but no less urgent message. Namely, information, informational labor, and information technologies were essential to heal a wounded but still dynamic capitalism. Schiller's research in *Who Knows* showed that a set of key structural changes caused by interstate, intercapitalist wars of position within the new information economy began a process, still reversible in this first account, that appeared to have engendered a new informationalized international division of labor to support a transnational corporate order. He recognized that the newness of the situation would cause some of his more speculative conclusions to turn out to be false. But the only false move in *Who Knows* was Schiller's report, true at the time, on the basic structure and key players of the computer/information technology industry, which changed almost completely (excepting IBM) with the emergence of the operating software monopoly, Microsoft, and the huge mass-producers of personal computing gadgets (IBM, Compaq, Dell, Hewlett Packard, and so on). Despite that, a few years later, when he finished *ICE*, Schiller was already more certain about his research and, tellingly, curbed some of his more optimistic views on the possibility of arresting the restructuring processes via deceleration.

Schiller began *Who Knows* in the late 1970s and published it in 1981. The late 1970s were probably the years of the most intensive research Schiller did in preparation for both *Who Knows* and *ICE*. However, it is important to recall that Schiller had already initiated his study of information resources and distribution in the 1960s, and had pursued details about the informational apparatus since then to an increasing degree in each new phase of work. Information enclosures were, after all, consequences of the military-industrial attempts to control the generation and distribution of information-communication resources that he had documented in *MCAE*, *The Mind Managers*, and *CCD*. Schiller also noted that he had fortuitously been made more conscious of a number of dynamics already beginning to take form in the 1970s, in particular computerization, privatization, and commoditization of information. Here, he acknowledges the influence of Anita Schiller, who, because of her work as a research librarian at the University of Illinois in the 1960s, and in the 1970s at UCSD, was alert to issues associated with new information technology. Libraries, and librarians, have served, in a sense, as the canaries in the society's informational mines, signaling the presence of harmful conditions before the rest of the society can perceive them. Schiller attributed to Anita his "recognition and partial understanding of what was occurring" in the political economy of information—privatization being the most pressing problem. "No one," he said, "has paid closer attention to and analyzed this development more thoroughly than Anita Schiller" (*ICE*, vii; see also *Living in the Number One Country*, 39–41). *Who Knows* is dedicated to Anita Schiller, and their common interests are lovingly remembered in *ICE* as an engaging dialogue "carried on daily, during our walks by the ocean and our nightly promenades through the vacant streets of La Jolla" (*ICE*, vii). Finally, the Schiller's sons were by now involved in their own professional pursuits, but never failed to contribute to the effort. They were, as always, "involved at every stage of the project, discussing the basic conceptions and giving me their thinking, as well as criticizing my own" (*Who Knows*, viii).

That solidarity stretched from La Jolla to the ever-widening community of colleagues and friends in Latin America and Europe, whose influence and help Schiller warmly acknowledged during this period of writing. This intellectual activity overlapped with Schiller's international activism to achieve a nondominating information and communication order. Accordingly, a number of scholars, already mentioned in relation to the New World Information and

Communication Order (NWICO) debates, were important to Schiller's think-
ing during the writing of *Who Knows* and *ICE*, including his friends at the
Latin American Institute for Transnational Studies (ILET) in Mexico City—
Juan Somavia, Fernando Reyes Mata, Noreen Janus, and Rafael Roncagliolo.
Also mentioned was Cuban writer Enrique González Manet, whose work on
the information society was very important in this period. Schiller's friends,
Kaarle Nordenstreng and Cees Hamelink, were thanked for their input into
this research effort, as were his colleagues and friends at the University of
Stockholm, including Karl-Ole Nilsson, Jan Ekecrantz, Nils Hugo Geber,
Göran Hedebro, and Margareta Ingelstam. Schiller wrote much of *Who Knows*
in New York while he was a visiting professor at Hunter College-CUNY in
1978 and 1979, where he recalled having helpful and engaging discussions with
his friends Stuart and Elizabeth Ewen, whose own critical histories of advertising have helped advance understanding in critical communication studies of
the political economy of culture and communication.

The refinements and distinctions of *ICE* were influenced by another set of
colleagues and friends, among whom the British sociologist Frank Webster was
probably the most important. Webster was inspired by Schiller's attempts to
see through the hype and futurology surrounding information-communication
technology and deal with the more fundamental processes of labor, commercialization, and social control. He was also deeply involved in a project similar
to Schiller's that challenged the dominant uses and representations of new
information technology, which led to the research published with Kevin Robins in the book entitled *Information Technology: A Luddite Analysis* (1986). Like
others before him, he was inspired by reading Schiller and, by 1980, began to
correspond with him. Schiller liked what Webster had to say and invited him
to UCSD as a visiting professor in 1981 through 1982, the year Schiller began
writing *ICE*. In addition to this intellectual encounter, also very productive for
Schiller's thinking about the issues he wanted to confront in *ICE*, were contacts
with his friends and colleagues in Tampere, Finland, especially Leena Paldán,
and in Paris, where he wrote much of the book while a visiting professor at the
University of Paris (VIII). Among these influences were Michèle and Armand
Mattelart, Bernard Miège, Patrice Flichy, Seth Sieglaub, and other writers in
the political economy of communications area, including the Uruguayan
scholar Roque Faraone.

It was coincidentally during this period that three young scholars, all born
at the end or soon after World War II, decided to put together a collection of
essays to honor Schiller, entitled *Communication and Domination*. Two of these
were Leena Paldán and Göran Hedebro; the third was German political scien-
tist and communications scholar Jörg Becker. It was time, they thought, that
Schiller's many contributions to "a radical humanistic theory of democracy" be

recognized for providing energy and motivation "for critical communication scientists all over the world" (Becker et al. 1986, viii–ix). By then, Schiller's work had been translated into about a dozen languages, influencing critical scholars from "socialist or capitalist, developed or underdeveloped" countries. The essays that Becker, Paldán, and Hedebro collected for this festschrift represented work from a number of academic fields to show the interdisciplinary reach of Schiller's ideas, including economics, political science, sociology, psychology, journalism, and cultural studies. Many of Schiller's old and new friends and colleagues wrote on topics that were at the center of his concerns. The book was, as its editors wrote, "First and foremost . . . a thank-you to Herbert I. Schiller [and also] a public dialogue with him" (Becker et al. 1986, ix). The book surprised Schiller, who hadn't seriously contemplated the degree to which his work actually influenced or inspired so many people. Of course, he knew that his work was well received in many quarters and hoped it was useful for the many initiatives and struggles people were involved in, but there was something a little discomfiting for Schiller about a book turning the spotlight on him. The quality and respectful way that this collection of essays represented him was not the problem. It was rather Schiller's own reluctance to make a big deal out of his work. (As I said in the introduction, I don't think he would have much liked the present book taking him as its subject matter either.)

What was more important to Schiller at the time was the acceleration of the commercial-governmental enclosures around public information. Schiller's task in *Who Knows* and *ICE* was to formulate a clearer understanding of how these enclosures formed part of the restructuring of the international political economic system. Throughout the 1970s, it became clear to Schiller that the restructuring of national economies in the advanced capitalist world had enlarged the role of transnational corporations and heightened the strategic importance for commercial interests of information-communication and information technology (with a few variations of social actors, these changes largely confirmed his earliest theories and analysis). In *Who Knows*, he set out to document these changes and suggest how we might interpret them, leaving some room for positive refunctioning of information technologies on the condition that a policy of deceleration guide their implementation. Here is a summary of the chapter themes in *Who Knows*:

Chapter 1, "Whose New International Economic and Information Order?" explains how information and information technology—telecommunications, computer, audiovisual, and data flows, and so on—became a strategic piece in competing national economic policies during the 1970s and early 1980s. Rivalries brewed between the United States and Western Europe, where ruling groups were moving to elevate new information technology enterprises and newly informationalized yet old industry sectors to a strategic position in the global economy. European leaders hoped to dislodge the U.S. business system from its hegemonic position and gain a strong foothold in the new international order. The United States responded with greater outlays in R&D, driven by increased demand from the Pentagon for high technology weapons, again using the war against socialism and Third World insurgency as a pretext. This push was supported by American diplomatic and academic efforts to stipulate U.S. leadership in information technology as an established benefit of comparative advantage, according to which all rivals were depicted as better off not trying to do what the U.S. does best.

As we have seen, the media represented these efforts as a natural progression of the modernizing forces of capitalism, grossly misrepresenting what for Schiller were the consequences of these apparently internal matters among interstate rivals. The first consequence was the extension of the technical base needed for managing the operations of transnational corporations; the second was the incorporation of the global workforce into this transnational system. The interstate rivalries added another dimension to these changes. In the process of vying for positions of strength in the information economy, there was a certain revitalization of the colonial system generated as each core state sought to entice the leadership of former colonies into the new international division of labor (NIDL). This regionalization of the NIDL, connecting the global workforce via widening and overlapping hub-and-spoke networks, came to structure the direction of asset flows (informational resources, capital, labor productivity, strategic information, and so on) in the new economic order. This pattern benefited the transnational enterprises. It fostered the U.S. economy's decentering and most national states' demotion to the role of support team for colonization of databases and labor in the emerging global network. Nevertheless, the United States remained crystal clear about what its position should be among the dominating countries and moved to secure it.

Chapter 2 offered a glimpse of "The Infrastructure of the 'Information Society,'" by identifying top transnational corporations (TNCs) headquartered in the new informationalized order's number one country. This report was accurate as far as it went, but Schiller's snapshot description of major players would soon fade, as certain details were made irrelevant when new and more aggressive entrants took over the information technology field. A couple of general structural points have nevertheless been proven correct. First, he clearly saw the strategic importance of databases and database-operating software for a range of newly informationalized global operations (insurance, banking, accounting, airlines, etc.). He also explained the historical trajectory of the microelectronics entrepreneurs of the 1950s and 1960s, who took advantage of the military-induced demand for information technology to transform their small companies into highly capitalized corporations by the 1980s, creating barriers of entry along the way for smaller participants. The focus on political-economic context and socially determined uses helped inform the historical understanding of new technology. The trend has remained much the same, and by comparison with his figures that showed a start-up firm paying upwards of $100 million to get into the microelectronics business in the 1980s, as opposed to $5 million in the 1960s, we can cite the recent example of IBM's investment of $3 billion to build a modern, high-volume microchip facility in New York state in 2002.

Although Schiller could be faulted for not predicting who the new industry leaders would be in the coming years, he was nevertheless quite prescient in detailing who was at risk of becoming informational "have-nots" and how information inequality was an essential feature of the new order. As chapter 3 of *Who Knows* shows, this inequality was caused by "The Privatization of Information," not only in the peripheral countries inducted into the NIDL, but within the core as well, where commoditization of information was transforming once freely available, socially productive informational resources into salable goods for the private enhancement of paying customers' lives and businesses. Here he tracks the story of privatization after World War II, when the U.S. government began a number of initiatives to ensure that publicly funded production of information and information technologies would end up primarily in private, corporate hands. Among these initiatives was the government give-away of military-led R&D to private corporations and government hiring of research consultants whose proprietary claims on their reports helped to keep vital information out of public reach.

Decades of conservative U.S. leadership depicting privatization as a way to make government more efficient succeeded in removing information from widely available, easily accessible sources that had played an important role in American democracy. This impact of informational privatization is evident, for example, in the expansion of commercial databases adopted by public and university libraries as well as in the serial efforts of U.S. administrations to cut back the work of the Government Printing Office and, with it, the depository library system in the United States—the "facilities of democracy," as Schiller called them, that archive government reports, research, and indexes of all government publications *(Who Knows,* 66). Schiller added a note of hope to this story, suggesting that social protest may erupt against the privatization trend, and that within both government and industry there were countervailing forces, including interagency disputes in government bureaucracies and small competitors in the information technology business who emerged to fight against informational monopolization.

But while Schiller found hopeful signs in these disturbing trends, he still concluded that informational monopolies were awesome foes with powerful corporate-military-government-academic ties. Chapter 4, "The Corporate Media: Appropriation of New Communication Technologies by the *Fortune 500*," details how a new wave of system-serving audiovisual material was beginning to appear to assure greater control over the consciousness-shaping process taking place inside the walls of corporate culture. Schiller documents the way new video technologies have been used to create in-house productions to help corporations, especially in oil, energy, and other polluting industries, to counter public information about their operations that their employees and stock holders receive from a sporadic, negative news report in the mainstream media. Corporate expression was given a legal boost as well in the late 1970s with two Supreme Court decisions granting corporations speech rights equivalent to those of individuals (the 1978 Bellotti and 1980 Con Edison decisions; more on this in the following chapter). The in-house productions, with dedicated distribution systems, would soon move into new public outlets on cable television to take advantage of this new legal environment. The proliferation of infomercials we see today is an inheritance of these technical and legal changes.

In addition to audiovisual flows, the new order was completely dependent on voice and data flows—that is, information for managing far-flung operations' accounting, payroll, financial transactions, personnel, and so on. Chapter 5 is called "The *Fortune 500* and the International Flow of Information: Transborder Data Flows and the Global Integration of the World Business System." Transborder data flows were barely understood at the time Schiller wrote this, mostly because they were so hard to track, not just in technical terms but because the information was treated as the property of transnational firms and therefore as secret. This underscored yet again the meaning of the book's title—those who know what key economic information is out there are the major TNCs, and few others. This dimension of privatization and commoditization should be troubling for all those involved in efforts to create nondominating systems, suggested Schiller. There is too much that can be hidden that directly affects national economies trying to sustain, for example, equilibrium in currency markets, fair international negotiations involving geological surveys of primary resources in their territories, just labor contracts, personal data protections (data privacy), open discussions on military matters and surveillance technologies, and so on. Proprietary transborder data flows, enabled by the U.S. technological advantage, confront directly the viability of national sovereignty as a framework of international policy-making.

Chapter 6 explores another problem for national sovereignty as "Planetary Resource Information Flows: A New Dimension of Hegemonic Power or Global Social Utility?" Schiller returned to the study of how satellite technologies diminished the power of national governments, the only political entity strong enough to restrain TNC activities. As always, Schiller attempted to de-expertize the discussion of high technology, picking for this investigation the arcane applications of remote sensing satellites to show their dominating function. Various private groups have constituted a controlling complex of remote sensing capabilities that override interests of national governments. One group, Geosat Committee, Inc., sponsored by over a hundred U.S. energy and mining companies, university geophysical research units, and U.S. government-military operations (NASA, for example), has played a major role in privatizing remote sensing information. Industry participants in this "nonprofit" consortium pay upwards of $30,000 for a snapshot of "hyperspectral data" of the earth's "hard to find" oil, mineral, and vegetation resources (www.geosat.com; Koger and Dodge, 1998).

The last two chapters of *Who Knows* wonder "Who Needs Computer Communications?" and whether "The Insecure Foundations of the *Fortune 500's* Information Age" will impede the momentum of the new information economy. Schiller was always amazed at the ease with which technology was promoted without provoking debates about need. Do we really need computers, or does business need us to accept them in order to increase the productivity of the already overworked working people? Do we need answering machines (do we really need to hear from all those people), or is the gadget merely a way to force new spending on electronics? Do you have to have a cell phone (are there really that many important calls), or do the electronics and telecommunications industries need you to have it in order for them to extend their influence over your nonwork time? What you answer contributes to the balance between mind management and socially productive resource distribution, suggested Schiller. When he wrote *Who Knows*, there were only about a half a million computers in the United States. Today, over one billion have been distributed worldwide, and that's just counting personal computers. Who needs computers? Seventy-five percent of all PCs today are located in workplaces, and it's not clear if the 25 percent in homes aren't also being used for work. Almost 40 percent of the billion PCs are in the United States, 25 percent in Europe, and around 12 percent in the Asia Pacific region. The biggest users worldwide continue to be military and the transnational corporations (Kanellos 2002).

Were there any signs of weakness in the U.S. military-TNC industrial complex? First, Schiller returns to the problems inhering in the international system that could cause some setbacks to the creation of a new order led by the United States. The new rivals in Europe and Japan were making claims on the new international division of labor; much of the Third World leadership still demanded equitable conditions; and internal domestic strife could cause further political and economic shifts. Schiller excluded from this list the "socialist sector of the world economy," a traditional source of opposition in the international arena, because by 1980 it had become powerless to play more than a reactive role, and was being "pulled into the international market economy . . . to act as a stabilizer [rather] than as a source of disequilibrium" (*Who Knows*, 154).

With the socialist grouping out of the picture, the most insecure foundation of the information economy was inside the capital-state "common-front." One particular area of tension had been created by European Union (EU) leaders, in partnership with West European industries, to create data-protection laws that threatened profit-making of noncomplying national and multinational firms. The prospect of such laws, which are today in place throughout the EU, challenged the U.S. "free flow" doctrine and threatened global data flows of many American industries that do not have to comply with any serious data protection laws in the U.S.

The Third World leadership had yet to confront the issue of transborder data flows in this period, still focusing their response to TNC expansion on audiovisual goods. Moreover, the worsening economic conditions facing the Third World leadership and the Movement of Non-Aligned Nations had weakened their resolve to challenge the informationalization of the world system. Schiller recalled in this context the looming disjuncture separating the interests of ruling groups and peoples in the Third World. Schiller assumed that ruling groups would perceive incorporation into the informationalized NIDL as a way to jump-start development within the new economic order. In response, he could only urge caution, again arguing for deceleration of technology transfers as he had in *CCD*. In *Who Knows*, he also raised the possibility of temporary disassociation from the international market as an alternative for not-yet industrialized countries seeking to improve their chances of survival in the world system (disassociation, or autocentric development, was, after all, the defining feature of successful national economic policies in nineteenth-century America, Japan, and Germany; see Senghaas 1980). Schiller borrowed the idea of disassociation from the work of Cees Hamelink, whose research on national communication policy would be published in an important 1983 study called *Cultural Autonomy in Global Communications*. There, Hamelink built on the research of economic historian, Dieter Senghaas, in order to outline a neomercantilist framework of autocentric development for nondominating international communication policy.

So, besides the interstate disputes over transborder data flows and control of the NIDL, only the internal contradictions within the core capitalist economies remained to interrupt the progress of informationalization. Technology induced lay-offs and automation, and other features of the informationalized production process held the potential to cripple the system, Schiller suggested, as did the unceasing spiral of inflation and the industrial despoliation of the environment.

All of these themes return in *Information and the Crisis Economy*, though in a much more precise and confident style—confident because much of the speculative analysis in *Who Knows* had been confirmed by developments in the international political economy by 1984. By that time as well, the pace of change had quickened significantly, and Schiller's writing in a sense reflected that sweeping movement with well-practiced, rapid-punching arguments built on the foundation of research from *Who Knows*, as illustrated here by Schiller's chapter titles in *ICE*:

1. "The New Information Technologies Combat the Western Economic Crisis"
2. "Communication Against an Insurgent World"
3. "Information and the Push for Privatization and Productivity in the U.S. Economy"
4. "The Developing Crisis in the Western Free Flow of Information Doctrine"
5. "The Political Economy of Communication: Culture *Is* the Economy"
6. "Paradoxes of the Information Age"
7. "The Prospect for Democratic Communication"

The "crisis economy" of the title referred to the period of economic stagnation in the world system that set in during the late 1970s and early 1980s. This was exacerbated by spiraling inflation and double-digit unemployment in most of the advanced industrial economies (disproportionately affecting people of color in the large industrial-metropolitan zones) along with mounting debt accumulation in the not-yet industrialized periphery. Western leaders became gloomier about their economies' futures, and hence more insistent about the centrality of information technology in a revitalized global capitalism. The opposition to the world economic order—protagonized by UNESCO, the Movement of Non-Aligned Nations, and others in the 1970s—had succumbed further to the pressures and strains of economic trauma. Third World leaders were either being co-opted for the NIDL or rendered irrelevant by the unyielding power of a crisis economy and/or Western military threat. Schiller's analysis in turn became less hopeful. Yet despite or perhaps because of the amount of distressing evidence he found, Schiller's writing in *ICE* was more buoyant than in *Who Knows*. As we might expect, *ICE* spoke with assurance to a politically and intellectually interested reader engaged in challenging the status quo; it ends accordingly with a report on existing prospects for democratic communications.

Schiller condensed much of the detailed descriptions of *Who Knows* into statements in *ICE* such as this one: The new international division of labor, he said, "is not being effected according to a global plan or a specifically drafted design. It is proceeding rather under the impetus of countless institutions, state and private, international and local, with the chief decision-makers and influence wielders being transnational corporations" (*ICE*, 52). TNC power was succinctly explained as dependent on the NIDL and global marketing/advertising. The NIDL, once begun, was sustained by information technology and three sorts of informational flows: data (including voice), audiovisual, and surveillance. Likewise, global marketing research and transnational advertising were contingent on the placement and smooth functioning of these same flows. And again, all these flows were made feasible by the instrumentation of globally networked digital telecommunications that followed national states' acquiescence to the U.S. trade doctrines of "barriers down" and "free flow of information."

ICE continues with a concise analysis of the privatization trend in European communications systems, the latest affected countries then being Italy, Spain, and France. But the process was already moving northward throughout the European public service zone. Learn from the U.S. experience, Schiller seemed to be saying, and halt this troubling trend of privatization. Learn how the advertising-saturated cultural environment had encouraged unthinking consumerism in the United States with dire effects on Americans' nutrition and health. Who needs advertising? Not the ordinary citizen, but the goods' manufacturers and promoters. And consider that TNCs create global markets by turning national citizens into global consumers and sorting them according to market criteria. Moreover, when media systems are forced to compete for TNC advertising dollars, they make the legitimacy of the "free flow" doctrine much harder to contest.

Schiller also perceived how the "free flow of information" doctrine was being modified to serve TNC needs in the late-twentieth century. Free flow was always a swindle, and here again Schiller showed us why. He explained that U.S. businesses originally sought strength in the name of "free flow" but ended up creating the vulnerabilities to their continued command over the system. Schiller pointed out the contradiction that information flows could not literally be free if the U.S.-based multinationals expected to protect their proprietary claim on informational assets. Schiller suggests that in order for the U.S. economy to continue to reap the benefits from privatizing informational resources in a "free" informational market, they needed a U.S. trade doctrine that protected information as private property. Following Schiller's argument in *ICE* thus can help us understand how the present intellectual property doctrine became a centerpiece of U.S. trade policy, offering legal protection of U.S. business enclosures around global informational resources while also promoting free trade of American informational-cultural goods in the global market.

As noted already, two themes form a bridge to *Culture Inc.*, Schiller's third major writing effort in the 1980s. These were the mounting political-informational repression in the U.S. and the relation of political economy to culture, which he treated as interdependent. *ICE* and *Culture Inc.* were distinguished by Schiller's attempts to warn readers of the "growing separation of American thinking from international realities" that created "a perilous atmosphere for the time ahead," in which Americans would be "unable to comprehend or sympathize with the most elemental and powerful feelings and social movements of this era" (*ICE*, 109). This was a paradox in a country in which people were told they lived in the most technologically advanced, most information-media-rich environment on the planet. This paradoxical situation had a number of causes, among which Schiller identified the following:

- Private U.S. information controllers virtually "sealed off" Americans from world opinion and exposure to conditions of those less fortunate than them, which impoverished Americans' ability to cultivate an ethical regard for other peoples.
- This was reinforced by the class identification of a very large portion of the population—the so-called middle class—with the wealthiest fraction of Americans. And although they could not share the privileges of the rich, this middle stratum of Americans did have access to a relatively high level of material well-being that made it hard for them to "recognize, but much less empathize, with a huge, have-not world."
- Finally, Americans simply did not have the historical memory of World War I and II, which devastated Europe and parts of Asia and Africa. Many Americans therefore tended to have a restricted vision of the resource and infrastructural ruin of war, associating it instead with a prior time of prosperity, growth, and corporate and individual enrichment.

"The consequences of the already great and still growing divergence between American and world sentiment on fundamental issues of peace and social change, can hardly be overstated," Schiller concluded (*ICE*, 109). This was a stark vision of Americans' misunderstanding of their own cultural condition in the world. Schiller argued that this perilous situation would be sustained as long as American culture (and by extension, American national identity) was represented day in and day out—status quo ante and a posteriori—as the best possible one to have, the one others most wish to have, and the one that deserves worldwide admiration. This persistent problem—Schiller wrote this almost two decades ago—was certainly brought home to many observers on September 11, 2001, when we began to hear the chorus of Americans asking, "Why us?"

Schiller had endeavored in many ways to answer that question since he began writing in the 1950s, but in *ICE* he argued emphatically that the way to understand why Americans are clueless is through the critique of the political economy of culture. Such a critique, he said, must begin with a refutation of the widely accepted view that culture and cultural identities are separate from economy and politics. As he put it: "The separation of culture, politics, and economics is now absurd" (*ICE*, 81). The next step in understanding American cluelessness was to analyze a set of interrelated features of the information-based economies that delimited the sources, the mechanics, and the relationships of the informational and creative cultural processes. An additional step was to recognize alternatives by which we may determine what direction to take for achieving a nondominating system. For that, said Schiller, we must begin with an elementary question: *"What kind of a society do we want to live in?"* At the very least, this question opened up thinking to the possibility that alternative conditions could exist, to different choices for developing human potential, and to the idea that we can take action to change an "otherwise menacing social order, propelled by a technology increasingly removed from public accountability" (*ICE*, 79). In Schiller's political economy of culture, there was no development out of reach of "human intervention and, if necessary, resistance" (*ICE*, 80). We will see how he elaborated this political economy of culture in the next chapter.

This chapter has discussed Schiller's investigations of the political economy of information and the deceptive claims of information age proponents. It examined how Schiller connected the deepening social stratification in America to the unequal distribution of informational resources. There were deepening fissures between information "haves" and "have nots," an analysis that Schiller would broaden yet again with his 1996 book *Information Inequality*, discussed in more detail in the concluding chapter. But it was *Culture Inc.* that marked the culmination of decades of research and writing on these matters. As such, that book has had a lasting ability to define the questions of media power in our own times. It is a book many consider to be Schiller's masterpiece, an achievement that the following chapter can only begin to trace.

Chapter Six

Culture Incorporated

> Whether the opportunity appears to create a new political movement that will press to change the underlying economy in a significant way and whether that movement will take up seriously the media-cultural issue are beyond prediction. What can be said is this. The possibility of a new social orientation in the United States—which will influence the world at large as well—is dependent on what happens to the national informational-cultural condition.
>
> —Herbert Schiller, *Culture Inc.*, 174

Schiller observed that by the end of the 1980s, "the shift to the right" in American society had been "extraordinary." He argued that much of the trend could be explained by decades of "expanding influence of the private business corporation," which had "tipped the balance of democratic existence to an uncomfortable precariousness" (*Culture Inc.*, 3; hereafter *CI*). Under Ronald Reagan's presidency, the U.S. government had abandoned virtually any appearance of support for programs to help working and poor Americans, replacing social virtues of the welfare state with market "virtues" of a national security state. The leadership continued to push the ever more aggressive "barriers down" policy across the planet as it spent the national budget into a record deficit in its effort to militarize the universe with "Star Wars" missiles and other weapons of mass destruction. With this shift to the right, the "entire political-cultural spectrum had shifted as well," allowing the "fringe right" to "dominate the columns and airtime of the mainstream media" (*CI*, 17). This situation made the writing of *CI* a significant event in the Herbert Schiller story. Though it was not his last work or last word on the issues that occupied his thinking since he began to write, it represented the culmination of the major lines of forty years of intellectual labor. It was also an eventful work of criticism for another reason. In *CI* Schiller confronted American anticommunism and the dark days of McCarthyism (for the first time in a substantial way) to frame his analysis of the "takeover of public expression" in late-twentieth-century America. He wrote as if the book were dedicated to all those who had ever fought and were still fighting antidemocratic attempts to take over information, public expression, and the means to produce public knowledge.

CI, as in all Schiller's previous writing, was addressed to a critically involved reader who desired to make a positive difference in the world—a reader who resisted being treated like a passive receptor of the already said, the already established routine, the already entrenched relations of power anchored in the class system. Its intellectual power was rooted in several fundamentals: a radical humanism that presumed people made history, made culture, and could make meaningful social change; a class analysis that presumed that the wealthy property-holding class would rather not have working and poor people make history, culture, or change—domestically or anywhere on the planet—and would use armed force, legal pressures, and political influence to get their way; Schiller's analytical holism that presumed that culture, politics, and economy had become interdependent in the twentieth century; and finally, the conviction that democratic and socially progressive visions of social needs and responsibilities should guide the distribution of cultural, informational, and material resources. Here is a sample of these fundamentals from *CI*'s introduction:

> Individual expression occurs each time a person dresses, goes out for a walk, meets friends, converses, or does any of a thousand routine exercises. Expression is an inseparable part of life. It is ludicrous to imagine that individual expression can be completely managed and controlled. Yet, no matter how integral to the person, it is ultimately subject to social boundaries that are themselves changeable but always present. These limits have been created by the power formations in society, past and present. I have tried to trace how some of these defining conditions have been established or reinforced in recent decades and what impact they have. The growth of private corporate power is seen as the prime contractor in the construction of contemporary boundaries of expression. . . . (6)
>
> [And yet,] It is not necessary to construct a theory of intentional cultural control. In truth, the strength of the control process rests in its apparent absence. The desired systemic result is achieved ordinarily by a loose though effective institutional process. It utilizes the education of journalists and other media professionals, built-in penalties and rewards for doing what is expected, norms presented as objective rules, and the occasional but telling direct intrusion from above. The main lever is the internalization of values. (8)

This internalization was made possible, though not necessarily guaranteed, by a weakening of the democratic order and the enclosures around information—a process that Schiller had spent half his life reporting on. This was the subject of a compact history in the first chapter of *CI*. Indeed, chapter 1 enacts one of Schiller's proposals for a nondominating cultural environment: what we might call his critical vigilance against forgetting. In "Weakening the Democratic Order," Schiller illustrated how historical memory can be refreshed so that past experiences distorted by the dominating culture can be reinterpreted and mind management rendered harmless (see also *CCD*, 88). It is worthwhile to consider the way Schiller assailed this "structurally induced amnesia."[1]

First, Americans were kept in the dark about their political and cultural condition by an abiding fear of alternatives to the American system, a fear induced by the specter of an awesome world communist menace that the U.S. leadership and compliant informational complex had manufactured. Schiller recounted how the culture of anticommunism in the number one country was experienced in various historical moments. Starting in the late nineteenth century, dissenters in America were stigmatized as anarchists, seditious aliens, terrorists, and communists. After the Russian revolution, these manipulative definitions were used to justify the bloody crushing of worker's movements for better wages and working conditions, making anticommunism America's de facto secular religion (cf. Herman 1990). Schiller recalled how the anticommunist witch hunts (carried out by HUAC—the House Un-American Activities Committee—, the FBI, McCarthy, and so on) worked effectively like a religious fundamentalist movement that sought to silence all dissent through several generations of playwrights, teachers, novelists, actors, journalists, and others.

This anticommunist mission succeeded in encouraging the vast majority of Americans to internalize "numbing acceptance of a political environment" in which unthinkable, antidemocratic, and antihuman forces could be depicted as normal and legitimate: for instance, mind-boggling amounts of military spending misallocating social funds for private corporate empowerment at the expense of hundreds of thousands of lost and damaged lives around the world; an embrace of technologies that facilitated hardly noticed expansions of surveillance and social control at home and around the world; celebratory depictions of commercial ownership of everything in the United States and everywhere else; a dying environment and rising rates of new diseases explained away as natural occurrences in modern life; a popular culture that encouraged laughter at derogatory jokes about other societies, especially those in the socialist part of the world, and so on.

Schiller concluded that after fifty years of military-led demand for industrial and intellectual output, the United States had become a national security state with a tightly controlled media-informational apparatus that kept Americans uninformed about the conditions that underlay their relatively prosperous existence. This deadening of American knowledgeability about the world around them reached "its apogee in the Reagan period, 1980–88" as the anticommunist witch hunt was turned on the U.S. government itself, and the neoconservative movement dismantled many social functions they labeled as bad "big" government, such as the one the "Reds" had in the Soviet Union. Schiller documented this devastation as the privatization or dismantlement of public informational resources, education, the welfare system, and attacks on other socially productive institutions, including the labor movement.

With alternatives either demonized or ignored, the corporate system became the only mode of economic organization Americans knew. Once this cultural condition was solidly in place, the system's failures, which occasionally erupted into public awareness with "some egregious corporate act" that the media couldn't ignore, could be blamed on one or two "bad apples" who, once gone, allowed the system to return to normal (*CI*, 20). As we have seen with the current crisis of the misleadingly labeled "corporate corruption" in the United States, Americans' inability to question the system, except in terms of emotional outrage, leaves them dependent on and vulnerable to corporate informational channels, which have done nothing but recapitulate the "one bad apple" story and thus "extricate [once again] the *system* from scrutiny and responsibility" (*CI*, 20).

How these informational channels have come to be saturated with the corporate message forms part of the subject of chapter 2 in *CI*, "The Corporation and the Production of Culture." In this chapter, however, Schiller elaborated a holistic analysis of the interdependence of economic, political, and cultural activities: "*All* economic activity," he said, "produces symbolic as well as material goods. . . . In fact, the two are generally inseparable" (*CI*, 31). He summarized decades of study on the uneven commercialization of creative processes and the devolution or absorption of the purposes of nonmarket cultural production into the commercial system, with the consequent transformation of social values into private-corporate values that serve that system. This chapter also updated previous work on the commercial system's tendency toward economic concentration and the antidemocratic outcomes that result from the "super-aggregations of resources in the cultural-informational sphere" (*CI*, 35). Schiller charged American media and communication researchers with neglecting this reality here again, though he was not surprised that academics mostly endorsed the values of the American business culture. Nevertheless, he found little cracks in this arrangement, in particular where the constant demand for a high volume of new diversions, entertainments, and story lines occasionally allowed an antisystemic message to seep into the general flood of information-cultural productions. But these were kept to a trickle by entrenched marketing criteria that informed executive decisions about what was made and, more importantly, what was distributed to the public (*CI*, 43).

Moreover, events in the history of corporate law helped to ensure that unruly, antisystemic messages would be submerged deeper into a widening tributary of corporate messages. In chapter 3, "The Corporation and the Law," Schiller extended his critique from earlier analyses of the Supreme Court decisions that defined corporations first as persons and then granted corporate expression the protected status accorded to individual expression. One of the most important features of Schiller's argument was that the Supreme Court's decision on corporate speech rights did not center on the nature of the source of expression but on assurance that expression itself was made available to the public. As he put it, "In general terms, it gave priority, if not preponderant weight, to the *rights of the recipient*—the receiver of the information and messages. This approach, whatever its intention, neatly redirected attention *away* from the message's source *to* the message's receiver" (*CI*, 52). In doing so, it disavowed the disproportionate power of corporations to control and direct the uses of informational resources that are available to the receiver, who is left with comparably little authority to demand that such resources be used for purposes other than those already firmly entrenched. This point of argument returned the focus of the essay to another dilemma having to do with dissent and protest in a culture wracked by anticommunist fundamentalism. As long as the conservative courts and government leadership see "subversion" in any popular challenge to American business culture, "receivers" can expect their civil liberties to take second place to corporate freedom (*CI*, 64).

Again, in search of countervailing forces, Schiller included in this essay some consideration of how contradictions might reverse the system-serving effects of this body of law, including rising dissatisfaction with advertising-saturated culture, especially as this affects both children's learning environments and the general population's health and nutrition. Still, he was concerned that efforts to limit commercial speech ran the risk of inviting increased state prohibitions on other forms of political and cultural expression. He suggested that this problem could be avoided if the debate about private-corporate power were redefined as a political issue about inequality of media access rather than a purely legal issue of speech rights. In that case, the American people, not the courts, could decide to correct the inequality and, by influencing the political process, demand that individual rights and liberties "be expanded as corporate power is forced to retreat." Schiller argued that the power of the people was a "potentially more decisive force" than either state or private-corporate power. The first step towards realizing this potential "people power" was "developing the political consciousness, which, in turn, minimally requires a new dimension of media access for those who are now systematically excluded" (*CI*, 64–65; see also McChesney 1999, 257–80).

Such minimal access remained elusive, however, as long as the law supported the growing presence of the commercial message in all spheres of public culture. In addition to legal advantages, there were other processes favoring corporate control of public expression, as Schiller pointed out in his studies of privatization in *Who Knows* and *ICE*. Continuing his research on "Privatization and Commercialization of the Public Sector: Information and Education," chapter 4 of *CI* offers another super-refined essay on the uneven but ongoing enclosures around public spheres of learning, democratic deliberation, and political expression. Again, to measure the stresses in the public informational sphere, Schiller examined the health and orientation of libraries, which by the end of the 1980s were thoroughly infiltrated by commercial informational features. Some resistance to commercialization still existed at that time, but, as we have seen in more recent years, public and university libraries have been thoroughly integrated with private commercial databases. The threat to society has remained the same: If market criteria determine library operations, then investments in, for example, database development, must provide pecuniary rewards to the owners of the database, or those investments won't be made. When asked what areas of public knowledge aren't worth investing in from a commercial standpoint, one corporate leader in the information sector answered, "Humanities" (81).

The pressures experienced by libraries were in no sense unique. Other "facilities of democracy" denied public funding and forced to depend on private, commercial sources also began to neglect unprofitable areas of cultural production and expression. In chapter 5 of *CI*, Schiller examines how this "movement away from public to corporate expression" extended into the "social landscape" where it infiltrated "developments in the arts, architecture, and the urban scene" (88). He explained how "the corporate capture of the sites of public expression" resulted from growing business image-enhancing patronage of the arts. Schiller described the increasing use of museum exhibits, art festivals, concerts, and shopping areas in urban and suburban landscapes for public relations purposes. This was the beginning of the temporal-spatial expansion of what we might call corporate advocacy marketing. Advocacy marketing aims to enhance the corporate image and create positive associations with corporate brands. As Schiller saw it, this corporatization of public expression enlisted intellectuals and artists dependent on patronage into system-serving cultural production, but in doing so created new vulnerabilities, since these groups were not predictable system advocates. He noted, however, that as yet he had found few signs that a critical mass of any significant counterforce was emerging from these arts and intellectual groupings.

The expansion of advocacy marketing accompanied privatization of public space, in suburban shopping malls for instance, and the gentrification of the inner city—"condominiums, boutiques, expensive restaurant scene"—that pushed out small neighborhood identities to make room for corporatized consumerist identities. Even in block parties of less affluent neighborhoods, corporate logos for beer and banks have increasingly become a familiar feature. Schiller summed up how advocacy marketing worked in all these areas, including with increasing frequency the space of public television. The result, he said, was that "the public's attention is focused on the corporation as social benefactor. Its actual dominant role as resource allocator for private interests is thereby more likely to escape the scrutiny it deserves" (106).

Moves to expand the territory of corporate expression not only shrank the nonprofit, nonconsumerist zones domestically, but as they extended across borders into "new markets"—that is, into other societies—the international public sphere also shrank. In "The Transnationalization of Corporate Expression," Schiller detailed some of the ways U.S. industrial restructuring, and other internal processes that have made commercialization and privatization possible domestically, had significant global impact. He focused on the period of deregulation of telecommunications in the United States—when "AT&T was 'mugged' by its *corporate-user* clientele" to create better cost options, flexibility, and borderless networks to serve transnational corporate needs. This case illustrated how much of the transnationalization that had occurred in the 1980s was not the outcome of a conspiracy or preplanned assault on public information systems worldwide, though the major players in the telecommunications and computer industries were well aware of what was at stake. It was rather a long, tortuous, litigious process in which the outcomes were hardly predictable. Even today, the telecommunications industry has not shown signs of stability since deregulation. What was clear was that once one country could provide transnational business users with unregulated, low-cost options, other countries would feel pressured to deregulate, or liberalize, their telecommunications systems. In other words, what national governments risked by protecting public monopolies was their economy's loss of transnational business to a rival country.

Where was the resistance in the international public sphere to this privatization pressure? Schiller argued that one site of resistance—limited as it was—had been UNESCO, where alternative approaches to the transnational deregulatory movement could still be nourished and defended. So Schiller was not surprised that the Reagan government had expressed extreme hostility toward UNESCO to the point of unilaterally withdrawing U.S. support (proportionally the most substantial) from that organization in 1984. This was the only international public forum in which poor and semi-industrialized nations stood on a relatively equal level in international affairs with the United States. Schiller argued that the U.S. withdrawal was a strategic move to "destroy the international public sector" and accelerate "deregulation and privatization in the international arena and in the poorer countries especially" (115). Deregulation served structural needs of transnational business—to protect commercial-informational flows, marketing, and uninhibited operation—and in the process abrogated national sovereignty. Once in place globally, the social consequences of deregulation already evident in the United States were bound to be repeated in some form. Advertising would expand in public media and cultural spaces, existing public services would be partnered with or replaced altogether by private-commercial services and organized according to market criteria, citizens would be (further) stratified into a hierarchy of consumers receiving needed "services," domestic sports and other cultural activities would be pressured to internationalize and commercialize for global distribution, and the electoral process would be further transformed from a deliberative one into a public relations and marketing effort to package and sell candidates.

Schiller ended chapter 6 with the words of Kenyan novelist and essayist, Ngugi wa Thiong'o on the effects of the "cultural bomb" of transnational capital to "annihilate a people's belief in their own names, in their languages, in their environment, in their heritage of struggle, in their unity, in their capacities and ultimately in themselves" (quoted in *CI*, 134). For Schiller, this was not just an effect of cultural imperialism from a core power to a peripheral nation, but was becoming the general condition in all areas dominated by the global business culture.

If the international forces of resistance were weakened or nonexistent, where would forms of resistance to the "cultural bomb" come from? Schiller turned to this question in chapter 7, "Thinking about Media Power: Who Holds It? A Changing View." Schiller examined what the learned opinion of media and communications theorists had to say about resistance to corporate power in the media. He found general agreement, despite a brief period to the contrary, that the media's "own material interests and imperatives" were less influential in shaping consciousness than "audience preferences" (136). There were three distinct yet uneven phases in this developing consensus.

The first phase was characterized by a tension between a domestic "limited effects" model and an international strong effects model, lasting for twenty years after the end of World War II. Both models were narrowly concerned with individual behavioral influences. Although Schiller did not make reference to his prior theorization of "institutionalized communication domination," we may note that his analysis of the domestic effects model showed how American communication research tended to reinforce the status quo by finding that audience selections, perceptions, and uses of messages were only partly influenced by the commercially-controlled media. In other words, there was little need for an explicit policy regulating the domestic system because of limited effects of corporate media on public consciousness. With minimal attention paid to corporate attempts to manage consumption and public knowledge, the domestic effects model also perpetuated a pluralist fantasy that a class system did not exist in the United States and that conflicts between the "haves" and "have-nots" over media-informational power were nonexistent as well. The international model, though based in the same research methods, found instead that strong media effects, if used strategically, could extend American influence and reinforce the informational power of U.S. media controllers. The research results showed strong propaganda effects fostered greater acceptance of American business culture abroad and helped legitimate the foreign policy goals of the United States. Promoters of this model candidly praised the ability of marketing methods to reproduce the core countries' consumerist system in the not-yet industrialized countries. While the existence of the class system was acknowledged in the international model, it was treated as alien to U.S. society (American exceptionalism), and anyway was said to have withered away globally after WWII with the spreading of American culture worldwide. Though Schiller marveled at the coexistence of these contradictory findings within the same research tradition, he was not surprised to find academic theories of media power used opportunistically to support corporate media power at home and U.S. foreign policy abroad.

The second stage occurred largely in the international communication field but also in the political ferment of rebellion throughout the world system. It was characterized by theoretical and institutional battles that pitted the dominant system-serving modernization/consumerism scholars against progressive cultural imperialism/counterculture scholars and activists. There was a short-lived reformist period during the mid to late 1960s and early 1970s when the latter group made some gains and powerful media were challenged by U.N. bodies, Third World nations, and activists in the United States who, for example, questioned the social agenda of the established media (children's advocates and activists from the black and Chicano movements fought for such reform domestically). Research in this period, Schiller's included, showed that media power domestically and internationally was bound up with economic-political power. This brief surge in critical thinking provoked modifications within the "limited effects" school as well, fostering acceptance, for example, of agenda-setting and gatekeeper theories within mainstream American communications research.

In the early 1970s, the reformist movement was already in decline, and by 1976, the Third World challenges had "crested," enfeebled by external economic trauma and deactivated within the bureaucratic limbo of "committees to study the problem." Organized international resistance was becoming rare, while acceptance rose for policies claiming that new information technologies were the key to modernization. (These problems were also addressed in *Hope and Folly: The U.S. and UNESCO, 1949–1985* [1989], a coauthored book with Edward Herman and William Preston). In the 1980s, media theory revived a notion of limited effects along two lines of argument. The first said that new technologies (such as VCRs and cable television) freed up the audience to become more actively involved in determining their menu of media items. This theory proposed the existence of an "active audience" that was technically savvy at creating "individualized viewing packages," and therefore free from the influence of dominating media (a view promoted in, for example, Ithiel de Sola Pool's apposite work *Technologies of Freedom*). The second line of theory came from cultural studies writers who proposed that meaning making was not a one-way message system but rather one in which an "active audience," made up of diverse cultural subgroupings, created a range of meanings, some of which were oppositional to the dominating media messages. One influential strand of this writing elaborated the theory of active meaning making as proof of audience power to resist cultural imperialism. Schiller noted that both these versions of "active audience" theory either minimized or completely disavowed the force of the class system and U.S. economic-military hegemony, instead emphasizing subjective and intersubjective experiences of television viewing. Upon such a pretext, it was theoretically feasible to deny the existence of strong media effects, the influence of disinformation and propaganda, and the reality of cultural imperialism.

Schiller had refuted the imperialism deniers in every book he wrote, but here he confronted the communications and cultural studies contingent. In the first phase of the growing consensus in audience power theory, the subjective powers of individuals obviated the need for understanding institutional or political economic power; at least that was the case in the domestic model. In the international model, by contrast, the embrace of media power was crucial, especially U.S.-led media power. But Schiller argued that in order to promote U.S. communication-media expansion, international communication theorists, in particular Daniel Lerner, failed to acknowledge American postwar imperial ambitions, instead depicting the new age of U.S. expansion as a benign process of development and modernization, with communication at the center of the purported project of global equalization. The second phase was a temporary challenge to this scholarly deception as activists, critical theorists, and international social movements revealed contradictory evidence showing persistent imperialist efforts in the world system and pushed for a new world information and communication order.

The third phase saw a resurgence of imperialism denial on a number of theoretical fronts in both the mainstream and in the field of cultural studies. This was not the first time Schiller entered a polemic in the communications field, but it was the first and last major textual confrontation he had with cultural studies in particular (which was enjoying growing legitimacy in communications and literature departments in universities throughout the United States at the time he wrote *Culture Inc.*). Schiller's task here could be described in general terms as one of recuperating a holistic analysis that did not presume culture, economy, and politics occurred in discrete or independent spheres of activity. More specifically, his polemic prepared the way for a longer discussion of resistance to the imperial system and its "cultural bombs" and where we might look to find nondominating sources of public expression in the coming crisis years.

For Schiller, denial of the historical evidence of imperialism—and its cultural-informational supports—or of struggles of resistance to powerful media was ludicrous. Of course, Schiller said, people have struggled to resist the system; of course, there have been no guarantees that the dominating message will succeed. As he wrote in *Culture, Inc.*, "The transfer of cultural values is a complex matter. It is not a one-shot hypodermic inoculation of individual plots and character representations" (149). But there were significant theoretical problems for Schiller at the base of work on active audiences—unfeasibility of aggregating subjective meanings from the full range of cultural experiences, or looking at television imagery exclusively to find (or disprove) cultural dominance, or assuming relative autonomy of social groups from the rule of market forces and capital domination over those forces, or displacement of class analysis with optimistic social pluralism, or ignoring environmental and health effects, among other cultural matters. Moreover, there had been a failing to explain how marketing, polling, and other surveillance features in the dominant cultural industries absorbed expressions of discontent in order to connect to the lives of spectators and consumers—indeed, marketing research showed some of the same concerns with subjective and intersubjective experiences as cultural studies (*CI*, 152–53). When such issues go unaddressed, Schiller argued, it becomes all too easy to accept that imperialism—social, cultural, or otherwise—is not the locus of media power.

As Schiller saw it, the best of cultural studies writing focused on class inequality (*CI*, 153–54). When attention to class became secondary to the exploration of TV viewing pleasures, for example, class became treated as an unwelcome reminder of a harsher reality (*CI*, 154). Despite efforts of some writers, cultural studies became better known for its idea that TV watching (or shopping) formed part of the active symbol-making work that goes into the formation of people's identities. While not all cultural studies writers endorsed the active audience trend, the latter still became—as Schiller recognized—somewhat more emblematic of the field. By 1999, an op-ed piece for the *Wall Street Journal* (Postrel, 1999) would describe it as the dominant trend in cultural studies, noting how "deeply threatening to traditional leftist views of commerce" the active consumer was, for it mirrored the right's idea that consumers get what they want from the capitalist system. She welcomed cultural-studies' betrayal of "the leftist cause" and its "support to the corporate enemy." More sympathetic commentators (Day 2002) have also identified the active consumer with cultural studies, summarizing essays in one cultural studies reader as reports on how "shopping was really a subversive activity" (cf. McChesney 1996).

While these unflattering accounts of cultural studies hound those who embraced the active audience idea, it should be emphasized that Schiller's critique of weak media power theory did not dwell on cultural studies in any significant way here or in subsequent writing, as some have suggested (Mosco 1996, 87). Beyond the objections noted above, Schiller found it much more significant that all versions of active audience writing (left or right) failed to explain the role of the "many-tentacled disinformation industry." For Schiller, the military-corporate-government enclosures around informational resources for over half a century remained the best evidence for explaining the "dismaying success" with which the big lies of the times were propagated. Among the falsehoods, Schiller included the Soviet menace, the hordes of third world revolutionaries, insurgents, and terrorists, and "the internal subversive character." "It is not a matter of people being dupes, informational or cultural," said

Herbert Schiller, on the set of "Herb Schiller Reads the New York Times," 1981. Courtesy of Paper Tiger Television, New York.

Schiller, in reference to one of cultural studies' widely circulated complaints about the theories of strong media influence. "It is that human beings are not equipped to deal with a pervasive disinformational system. Audiences do, in fact, interpret messages variously. They also may transform them to correspond with their individual experiences and tastes. But when they are confronted with a message incessantly repeated in all cultural conduits, issuing from the commanders of the social order, their capacities are overwhelmed" (*CI*, 155–56). For Schiller, a more vital question was how people could become fully informed to respond to the system *before* the occasional rupture of control occurred. Only by political means can that control be challenged, Schiller argued, not by waiting for a crisis to undermine the system, and certainly not by documenting the "individual's message transformational capability" (158).[2]

Schiller's argument that resistance, reform, or more significant systemic change depended on political action was further elaborated in the final chapter of *Culture Inc.*, "Public Expression in a Crisis Economy." The enclosures and hammer-like controls over the major informational apparatus, mighty as they are, have never achieved total blackout of alternative forms of expression or radical antisystemic communication. As we have seen, Schiller himself consistently directed his analysis and interpretation to those engaged somehow in making sure totalitarian attempts would be thwarted. This was his active audience—people who were already striving to make a difference in their culture work—from independent television and film producers to organizations and movements striving for social transformation—or were in the process of learning how to become cultural producers or "knowledge workers." He noted that when historical conditions had been ripe with organized resistance of large audiences, even small media have helped to make big revolutions, to paraphrase a study of the Iranian revolution (Sreberny-Mohammadi and Mohammadi 1995; *CI*, 168). Schiller also found hopeful signs in the way networked personal computers were beginning to be used as alternative means of communication, though he saw how insignificant they were inside a device that subordinated them to Pentagon, intelligence, police, and corporate "computational power." Schiller urged critical assessment of the alternatives in the context of this power.

The weakening of American dominance in the imperial system was certain to provoke new and unforeseen political activism with new and unforeseen, though predictably harsh, reactions from the military-industrial-government-entertainment complex. The sources of this activism would, as always, "be matters of jobs and living standards" as ever scarcer resources become the site of struggle, especially where the ruling groups tried to impose sacrifices "on those least capable of resisting them—the poor, the weak, the lower-income groups." We have seen in recent years how this political response to the system has grown into a worldwide movement for a radical overhaul of the global economic order. We cannot know how Schiller would have assessed this growing social movement, though he did make the comradely suggestion in *Culture Inc.* (170) that any future "efforts turned to gaining economic breathing space" would do well to remember "another vital ingredient of independence . . . [namely] cultural-informational autonomy." In his last decade of life, he argued that this struggle for cultural-informational autonomy has to begin at the center of cultural-informational control, the United States. The prospect for that struggle in the United States is the final issue to be addressed.

NOTES

1. This phrase is borrowed from Michael J. Shapiro's *Violent Cartographies*, 17.

2. It should be noted that critical cultural studies writers have also addressed these issues in an attempt to sustain a focus on one of the fundamentals of cultural studies: the articulation of public politics with the cultural-informational condition of working people (a point that Schiller himself acknowledged as a way to critique the classless vision of some "active audience" theorists). See, for example, David Morley 1993 or Andrew Ross 1997.

Conclusion: What Kind of Society?

If serious slippage does indeed occur in the United States' superpower role, the privileges accruing to this position soon will begin to disappear. . . . Ever more frequent rebuffs may be expected as the ability of the United States to achieve consent through coercion diminishes. . . . If in fact this occurs, many of the policies that the United States has pursued over the years will find support withdrawn, and unilateral actions to sustain American advantages in one or another part of the world may be too costly for a beleaguered superpower to exercise. . . . Whatever the social direction that a reduced world role induces, one outcome seems assured: a sharp increase in social conflict between domestic haves and have-nots, a struggle over shares of diminishing resources.

—Herbert Schiller, *Living in the Number One Country*, 199–200

Herbert Schiller retired as a full-time teacher at UCSD in 1990 at the age of seventy, teaching part time as emeritus professor until 1999. During this period he published over thirty articles and essays in various edited collections, journals, and periodicals around the world. First among the books he produced in this decade was the reissue of *Mass Communications and American Empire* (1992), which included his retrospective assessment of the global information-cultural condition. He also collaborated on several major new collections of essays, including *Triumph of the Image: The Media's War in the Persian Gulf—A Global Perspective* (1992), with George Gerbner and Hamid Mowlana; *Beyond National Sovereignty* (1993) with Kaarle Nordenstreng; and *Invisible Crisis: What Conglomerate Control of Media Means for America and the World* (1996), again with Gerbner and Mowlana. He also wrote about the role of informational stratification in the American crisis economy in *Information Inequality: The Deepening Social Crisis in America* (1996). His amazing energy only slowed at the age of seventy-four, and that occurred literally by accident when he was struck by a distracted bicyclist while crossing Washington Square in New York City. That was in the winter of 1994. His recovery was slow and never complete, though in that time he finished writing *Information Inequality*, continued to teach, and was fit enough to initiate another major writing project that would mix memoir and critical analysis in essays that he shaped into a book called *Living in the Number One Country: Reflections from a Critic of American Empire* (2000).

One attractive aspect of Schiller's work was his ability to perceive political economic processes that for most of us exist beyond the horizon of our experience. He would always bring the subject matter home, as it were, with his care for the cultural environment of the have-nots of the world. Schiller stood against the social harms caused by the corporate system, militarism, U.S. imperialism, and the media apparatus. These ethical and political commitments can be deeply disruptive of the particularistic, media-centered principles that define how journalism, media, or communications studies are generally taught. But a disturbance of the field's identity can also foster its renewal. This contribution to the profession is a part of Schiller's legacy. He strove to shift the balance of higher learning in media and communication studies—whether to be a knowledge worker or media producer—in favor of critical thinking and basic citizenship skills and away from an emphasis on technical know-how (in both research and media-making). Such a shift of emphasis bestows a serious social responsibility upon media, communication, and journalism teachers. Schiller put it this way: "Will those informed in communication theory and research continue to serve systemic power as so many of them have dutifully done over the last half century? Or will they apply their capabilities and talent toward critical assessment of the institutional structures now in place? Though a field's integrity, no less than the nation's well-being, is at stake, we cannot be confident of the answer" (*LNOC*, 126). This conclusion considers how we might take Schiller's work as a point of departure to meet this challenge in communication studies. We begin with the direct links between existing institutional structures and those Schiller examined.

There are many interesting continuities between his research and the issues that communication studies faces today, starting with the military-government-industrial complex. In chapters 3 and 4 of *Mass Communications and American Empire*, for example, Schiller wrote of the "militarization of the governmental sector" of communication that was taking place within bureaucracies directly linked to the White House. A fresh look at one bureaucracy that Schiller analyzed, the Interdepartment Radio Advisory Committee (IRAC), shows that it still has the power to recommend spectrum uses for the government sector, and that executive and military branches still hold disproportionate influence over those recommendations, causing weak public interest representation in the allocation and use of airwaves for social purposes.[1] The IRAC is now under the direction of the National Telecommunications and Information Administration (NTIA), which oversees federal spectrum management and advises the U.S. president on matters related to the communications infrastructure.

In addition to examining the militarization of spectrum allocation, Schiller also showed how military contracts bring a core group of private industries into a very exclusive economy of supply and demand that determines how communications, electronics, and information technologies are designed and produced, and how they function. Schiller found such a bureaucratic link between military and business interests in the Armed Forces Communication and Electronics Association (AFCEA), which is still working to put government and military needs at the top of the agendas of electronics, computer, and communications industries. Schiller quoted an AFCEA exhibitor's brochure: "Here is where industry really meets the men who know—prominent government and military leaders who have the power of decision" (*MCAE*, 103). Today the AFCEA's pitch is much the same. Its web site notes that among the

Herbert Schiller, New York City, 1997.

top ten reasons for corporations to become sponsors are reaching "government decision-makers and advisors," and gaining "market visibility as a 'player' in the C4, Intelligence, and IT industries doing business with the military and government. As one of our members said, 'If you are not visible in AFCEA, your status as a "player" is questioned'" (www.afcea.org/sponsors/top10.asp). The present group of AFCEA's sustaining sponsors continues to represent one-third of the top fifty defense contractors. These interlocking interests include many of the same companies detailed in Schiller's 1969 account, though, of course, new players have appeared in the time since Schiller wrote about the organization. One of the more important is The Carlyle Group, whose board members include a former defense secretary (Frank Carlucci), a former secretary of state (James Baker), a former FCC commissioner (William Kennard), and former president G. H. W. Bush (father of the current president). Also included in the top fifty are General Electric, the parent company of the National Broadcasting Corporation (NBC), and the Halliburton Company, headed in the 1990s by the current vice president, Dick Cheney.

These few examples illustrate how research into the power structure could be pursued following Schiller's leads. As he showed in all his work, such research identifies contemporary players, their positions, their outlooks, and their interlocking interests. However, Schiller also insisted that the insight we might gain from this research into the complex and the power elite would be limited unless we could layer into our analysis an account of how the complexes and the system are related—a procedure that moves the analysis from the particular to the totality of existing power arrangements. Schiller accomplished this in his first major investigations and writings by detailing attempts by leading military and corporate groups to shape the communication apparatus to their advantage, reinforcing and extending American military-economic hegemony in the twentieth century. By transposing Schiller's analytical moves in *Mass Communications and American Empire* onto the current political and economic situation, we can begin to suggest what the ruling groups have in mind for communications in the twenty-first century.

When Schiller first analyzed the process of integration and control of communication under military-corporate direction, foreign-policy was couched in a discourse of *counterinsurgency* to announce the aims of war in Vietnam. This and other military campaigns were part of a foreign policy principle of *containment* of communism around the world. Starting with the Reagan and the first Bush presidencies, this policy language began a shift away from *counterinsurgency* and *containment* toward *antiterrorism* and *preemptive military action* (offensive, first-strike warfare). As recent investigations have shown, a blueprint for this foreign policy shift was completed in the early 1990s by militarists within the first Bush administration who sought to advance American dominance in the wake of

Soviet communism's collapse.[2] A decade later, in the aftermath of the September 11 attacks on New York City and Washington D.C., antiterrorism became the term of art describing a new period of crisis management in the United States, while preemptive warfare came to define the essence of the second Bush administration's national security strategy. While all the consequences of the present crisis operations are not yet known, the following brief examples suggest some questions communication studies might ask at this time in order to assess what the systemic pressures on the American informational condition are and how these relate to trends identified by Schiller:

- The effect on the government information infrastructure of President Bush's *National Security Strategy of the United States of America* (United States, 2002; hereafter, *NSS*), an encompassing view of the White House's foreign and social policies "to defend the homeland, conduct information operations, ensure U.S. access to distant theaters, and protect critical U.S. infrastructure and assets in outer space" (*NSS*, 30). General points of information policy in the *NSS* address the administration's aim "to sustain our intelligence advantage" by retooling Cold War surveillance machinery to fight "international terrorism" (*NSS*, 30), while more specific points revive a familiar list of post–World War II and Cold War calls for "public diplomacy," "free flow of information" (*NSS*, 6), technological fixes for world poverty (*NSS*, 23), informational freedom in communist China (*NSS*, 28), and international communication to "help people around the world learn about and understand America" (*NSS*, 31).
- How national resources for education and public information are allocated and used by a system that operates a military enterprise—perhaps the largest centralized economy in history—built at a cost of $20 trillion (in FY2000 dollars) since 1946 (Center for Defense Information 2002, 35). The requested 2004 annual operating budget of over $400 billion represents "half of all the U.S. government's discretionary expenditure" and "nearly twice the defense spending of the next 15 of the world's military powers combined" (Borger and Teather 2003, np). This budget supports an infrastructure of bases, installations, and troop deployments in over 130 countries ("U.S. Military Might: The Facts"; Freedland 2002, np). This territorial backbone of U.S. imperial power depends on advanced global communications, the latest innovation including a new airborne information system that allows, "as never before," command and control communications to stretch around the world for coordination of U.S. forces engaged in multiple, simultaneous wars (Shanker, 2002, A8; see also "U.S. Military Bases and Empire").
- A clarification of the panoptic features of President Bush's Executive

Order for *Critical Infrastructure Protection in the Information Age* (October 2001), which established the "President's Critical Infrastructure Protection Board" (PCIPB) comprised of the upper crust of the military and intelligence bureaucracies.[3] In September 2002, the PCIPB issued *A National Strategy to Secure Cyberspace*, calling for volunteers of "teachers, military officers, privacy experts, doctors, stock brokers, police, civil servants, computer scientists, State government officials, corporate CEOs, and Federal officials" to watch internet usage for signs of terrorist activity (www.whitehouse.gov/pcipb).

- The impact on information resources and uses by the broad surveillance operations mandated in the omnibus law "Uniting and Strengthening America by Providing Appropriate Tools Required to Intercept and Obstruct Terrorism Act of 2001" (USA PATRIOT Act, October 2001). This act reorganized and expanded existing laws used to investigate suspected terrorists and those carrying out related "terrorist offenses," enlarging the power of the police, FBI, CIA, National Security Agency, and an ensemble of military intelligence agencies to conduct surveillance on all people residing in the United States. The integration of surveillance systems under the PATRIOT Act will only be feasible after achieving telematic "inter-operability," a key feature of the new information infrastructure requiring hardware and software engineering for instantaneous interagency database mining and profiling hitherto prevented by law or technical limitations.

- The changes in informational priorities of a number of established bureaucratic complexes instructed to achieve "inter-operability" of local, national, regional, and federal communication systems. For example, the NTIA manages an "interoperability" initiative through the offices of its public safety program (PSP) seeking "the voluntary adoption of user- and industry-developed technical standards to resolve barriers to interoperability" (Victory 2002). The Federal Communication Commission (FCC) has sponsored a corporate-military-government group called the Network Reliability and Interoperability Council (NRIC) to determine standards of "optimal reliability and interoperability" to "address the Homeland Defense concerns" (www.nric.org/charter_vi/index.html). The NRIC's 2002 membership list included military contractors, electronics-information-computer industry interests, and administration representatives such as the Commerce Department's Communications Critical Infrastructure Assurance Office.[4]

- Finally, what the purposes and designs of the new governmental information infrastructure will be once the establishment of the Department of Homeland Security (provisionally created in October 2001, finalized in

2002) completes the most massive reorganization of the government bureaucracy since the 1950s. The new department envisions full integration and interoperability of databases controlled by the twenty-two agencies that comprise it. In a parallel effort, the Department of Defense established the Total Information Awareness (TIA) system to integrate surveillance research and systems funded by the Defense Advanced Research Projects Agency (DARPA) (Mayle and Knott 2002). The TIA (renamed Terrorist Information Awareness in May 2003) was set up for data-mining "financial, education, travel, medical, veterinary, transportation and housing transactional records [as well as] face, finger print, and other identifying data," including body odors (http://www.darpa.mil/iao/TIASystems.htm). A related data-mining project called the Advanced Research and Development Activity (ARDA)—a Clinton administration initiative—has also been pursuing improvements of biometric and kinesics surveillance for the National Security Agency, Central Intelligence Agency, and the Defense Intelligence Agency (Markoff 2003, A20). Clarification is needed on what the TIA and ARDA systems and homeland security department will attempt as they integrate public and private information-surveillance databases and networks under military-government direction (see Miller 2002; Risen and Shanker 2002). Of central importance to communication researchers will be the long-term effect that these costly state-sponsored surveillance activities have on information technology R&D, the funding and freedom of critical scholarship, and the social conditions for democratic communication in the United States.

Schiller interpreted the trend toward hypercentralization of informational power—which, these examples suggest, is accelerating under the Bush administration—as contrary to the avowed logic of American democracy. He argued that the problems that flowed from this contradiction, as he analyzed it in nearly fifty years of work, were compounded when news media failed to routinely publicize and scrutinize military-government-corporate attempts to acquire control over information. This was the media's ideological function, a concern at the heart of Schiller's work on mind management. The question was how the informational apparatus, as he called it, along with the menu of domestic media content, supports the aims of U.S. military-industrial interests while serving up diversions for domestic American audiences. *The Mind Managers* provides a good point of departure for suggesting how critical ideas and research in communication studies can be generated for analyzing consciousness-shaping today.

To understand the continuities between *The Mind Managers* and our own time we need to acknowledge, as Schiller himself did in later writings, that the media–communications conglomerates he examined in the 1960s and 1970s are no longer strictly American but are global in intent, markets, and coordination of capital and labor. But, Schiller insisted that we keep in mind that the global reorganization doesn't mean a complete collapse of American cultural power or the importance of the U.S. market for international information-cultural businesses. With this modification in hand, the following questions are offered for the critical assessment of mind management today:

- How the increasing use of public relations to represent foreign policy shapes the public's consciousness domestically and internationally. Recent examples include the 2001 appointment of a former chairman of J. Walter Thompson and Ogilvy & Mather Worldwide as the Undersecretary of State for Public Diplomacy and Public Affairs, and the contracting of the PR firm, Rendon, in 2001 to manage perception worldwide of U.S. military campaigns in central Asia, South America, and elsewhere (Solomon 2001).

- How ongoing reductions of funding for public informational services, from libraries and government information sources to public education, affect public knowledgeability. Examples include a 2002 executive memorandum from the Office of Management and Budget ("Memorandum") that ordered the privatization of the printing operations of the U.S. government. According to the nonprofit group, OMB Watch, this act signaled the disintegration of a 140-year-old system that had successfully kept the public informed about government projects, reports, research, and the like (www.OMBWatch.org).

- The accelerated concentration of media ownership in the hands of private corporate enterprises, most of which are transnational entertainment conglomerates, and the role of the state and a powerful corporate lobby in this process. Examples include, among many others, passage of the 1996 Telecommunications Act and the Federal Communication Commission's forfeiture of public interest advocacy, most recently their inclination to eliminate all ownership restrictions, further privatize the public airwaves, and condone media concentration. Of equal importance is the media's failure to report these activities to the public; indeed, ranking number one on Project Censored's list of the top twenty-five censored stories of 2001–2002 was the FCC's effort to abolish ownership caps and foster commercial monopolization (Phillips 2002).

- How news media depict foreign policy aims and military strategy. Examples include evident compliance of major network and cable news with U.S. foreign policy aims between the U.S. invasions of Afghanistan in 2001 and Iraq in March 2003 (Fairness and Accuracy in Reporting 2001,

November and October, and 2003, March). Related examples would examine Hollywood studio heads' agreement to devote a certain amount of production to support U.S. security strategy and war aims after meeting with chief White House strategist Karl Rove, and President Bush's media advisor, Mark McKinnon in the fall of 2001 (Calvo 2001).

- How the trend toward concentration in the information-entertainment business demands intensive and centralized consumer surveillance, leading to parallel expansion and concentration of the marketing research industry. A good illustration is offered by the Dutch marketing research conglomerate, VNU, which not only owns most of the leading consumer surveillance companies in the world—including all major television audience, music sales, and shopper tracking firms—but has strategic partnerships with such large credit reporting corporations as Equifax in the United States (see Miller et al. 2001, 171–94). An historical study of the integration of surveillance systems suggests that the institutional ensembles examined in *The Mind Managers* interlock in ways that were not yet developed when Schiller presented his separate findings on the military-industrial controls over information and those controls under the direction of cultural conglomerates, polling, and advertising companies. This trend must also be examined in the context of the 2002 *National Security Strategy* and activities of the TIA, ARDA, and Department of Homeland Security.
- A final theme that could be drawn from *The Mind Managers* is an examination of the content and aims of media education and academic publishing in communications and information studies. How well are new generations of mind managers—media critics, producers, researchers, and scholars—prepared for understanding the above trends.

This list of current issues, limited as it is, raises questions of how ideological forces shape Americans' ability to know about and respond to the political and social realities of the day. As Schiller pointed out, if communication and media studies truly aim to inform and educate journalists and media critics, it cannot ignore the parallel ambitions within the power structure. "How paradoxical," he said, "that representatives of power have no difficulty with referring to domination, while so many communications researchers seem unable to utter the word!" (*LNOC*, 124). This was the outward orientation to the field that Schiller demonstrated in the themes of his scholarly publications. It was also implicit in the way he addressed students and teachers as people who cared, at a minimum, about the public interest, and who perhaps were even searching for a place to begin the critical tasks of social transformation. In his last writings, when Schiller spoke directly of the potential for change, he argued that the United States itself was starting to look like a place on the verge of major social upheaval. As we have seen, an important dimension of his writing was the effort he made to tie his analyses to the movement of history.

For example, in the final chapter of *Information Inequality*, "The 'Failure' of Socialism and the Next Radical Moment," Schiller revealed a long list of conflicts and symptoms of system failure that provided evidence to him of the imminent rupture from within the United States. Here, after all, is a society in which the abiding experience of consumerism had heightened awareness of consumerism's false promises, spectacular waste, and frenzy-inducing public culture. In a society where the word *stress* has general currency, sources of social breakdown are ubiquitous—the cost of living increases faster than per capita income, people overspend themselves into debt and work more hours to make up the difference, public education is underfunded, and risks of despair, marginalization, and ill-health are socialized, while physical and mental care are privatized. And freedom of speech, the right to dissent from this social arrangement, is doled out according to market criteria rather than public interest (*Information Inequality*, 139–40).[5]

Schiller observed these contradictions and paradoxes and wondered how long it would take for the military-industrial team to shore up defenses against the certain tide of dissent and social upheaval. On this point, he argued that the "character of the political administration in the immediate years ahead," while beyond prediction, already showed signs "that an all-too-probable rightist regime will impose heavy burdens on the weakest groups, while proclaiming its above-class, national goals." He had seen signs of this shift in the Reagan and the first Bush administrations, which he called the most reactionary to come along in fifty years. By the mid 1990s he noted the continuing rightward movement of the country's leadership, the locus of which was the Republican congressional majority, calling attention to its particular character with a reference to the phenomenon of "Friendly Fascism," identified by Bertram Gross in a book of the same name. The coming of an authoritarian regime in the United States was on the horizon, argued Schiller, who had demonstrated that its potential power resided in the coordination of U.S. military and the cultural-informational interests (*Information Inequality*, 140; *MCAE*, 37; see also Miller et al. 2001).

Nevertheless, Schiller said that while it was impossible to foresee the rightist regime's duration or the sources of its demise, it was evident to him that America contained "a wide pool" of "talented, knowledgeable, clear-eyed individuals of integrity, who could, under still-unforeseen circumstances, easily be engaged in projects that would offer a socially expanded perspective to the nation's deepening dilemmas and crises." In his estimation, these would be among the sources of the next radical moment (*Information Inequality*, 140–43). As he predicted, a new generation of Americans began to unite under the banner of a global justice movement, with efforts stretching from Seattle and Washington, D.C., to sites around the world—its momentum growing in 2002 and 2003 with dissent against the U.S. war on Iraq. Groups pressing for alternatives were linked by hundreds of Internet and small media initiatives, from posters and graffiti to community radio (for example, the Independent Media Center, Free-Speech TV, Direct Action Media Network, Fairness and Accuracy in Reporting, Media Channel, Project Censored, Free Media Network, and Pacifica radio stations).

Schiller did not live to see the emergence of the global justice movement, but his critical interest in resistance movements of prior decades gives us some idea of what he would contribute to the movement today. In those earlier periods of instability and rebellion in the 1960s and early 1970s, Schiller focused his energies on raising awareness of the informational-cultural issues that he thought were central to the transformational effort. The record of his thinking shows two distinct approaches to this critical labor. The first one concerns what he saw as the tasks for critical media research. The second approach was geared toward decision makers working to develop nondominating communication-cultural policies. This move from theory to practice can be illustrated by comparing two of his works from the 1970s.

In 1973, he proposed a list of what he considered the constituent elements of critical media research on the power structure. A few years later, in *Communication and Cultural Domination*, he outlined possibilities and vulnerabilities of a nondominating cultural-communication policy. Here are those proposals and suggestions, written at a time of international upheaval when 130 or so nations agreed that the global system was rotten and an alternative economic and informational order was needed.

A RESEARCH AGENDA FOR CRITICAL COMMUNICATION STUDIES

Decades before the loose talk of globalization began to dominate the news, Schiller understood that to be relevant, communication research had to account for the global scale of contemporary realities. In 1973, Schiller presented his proposal to an international workshop in a paper entitled "Mass Communication Research on the Power Structures of Society." In that paper, he named five issue areas for the work of critical communications research, which, with the addition of the military-informational complex, corresponded to his own scholarly investigations. They continue to be important aspects of power structure analysis today (quoted in Hamelink 2001, 12–13):

1. The extent of the local, national and international market organized by the multi-national corporations, as well as the character of the economic activity engaged in; i.e., extractive, heavy industrial, consumer or knowledge production. Related and equally significant data would have to be prepared on the social character and educational preparation of the labor force engaged in the enterprises.

2. An analysis of the structure of the mass media and the rest of the informational system in the areas dominated by the multi-national business units. This would include information on ownership, financing, and the evolution of all control mechanisms that are utilized in the media system.

3. An inventory of the ancillary informational and communications services/industries that serve as intermediaries between the multi-national corporations and the media system proper, either in the preparation of messages or in the preparation of audiences. These would include the market research and public opinion firms, the advertising agencies, the public relations companies, the business consulting agencies, the research institutes attached to business, government and academia.

4. The structure and organization of the educational and the para-educational systems and their connections with the corporate economy (wherever they can be determined). This suggests an analysis of the formal educational system with respect to size, adequacy and character of financing, use of materials, organization of curriculum, selection of instructional staff. On the para-educational side this requires a comprehensive scrutiny of such activities as the movie, radio, television, record and publishing industries, and the recreational games and comic book industries. Besides the character of the messages and their relationship to the structures processing them, the degree of penetration of private informational-recreational business conglomerates into national life, seem to be minimal areas for research inquiry [*sic*].

5. The mechanisms by which the "consciousness" industries and their messages and total environments are organized, packaged and exported to areas that are under the multi-national corporate activity umbrella. And, finally, an evaluation of the consequences of this penetration of social-cultural informational material on the developmental patterns of the areas affected.

TOWARD A NONDOMINATING CULTURAL-INFORMATION POLICY

Soon after he issued these proposals for research, Schiller considered the problems of creating alternative policies that were nondominating not just in theory but also in practice. In other words, research alone did not address the political dimension in which new communication and cultural institutions might operate. In *Communication and Cultural Domination* he envisioned a realistic policy that would be transitional—that is, one caught between old and new, and fraught with many contradictions and tensions. Most importantly, a nondominating policy or politics of communication and culture had to go to the heart of social conflict and have inscribed within it a critical awareness of basic social processes and class relations that had structured the international division of informational-cultural labor. In that sense, Schiller's suggestions assume the existence of an antagonistic imperial presence, or at least of powerful groups with imperial aspirations (this was, after all, written for those involved in policy debates on stemming U.S. cultural imperialism). Schiller offered no fixed and final answer for rethinking policy along these lines, but he did elaborate on the general character of a nondominating communications-cultural policy in *CCD*, the contours of which can be sketched out as follows:

1. The Western model is not appropriate for societies seeking liberation from the class system. It may be attractive, well equipped, and lustrous, but it should be examined thoroughly, dissected in every detail, before accepting it.
2. Communications-cultural liberation "is opposed to repressive authority and domination regardless whether it is exercised from within or outside the country. Defenders of the cultural status quo sometimes challenge external authority, but only in order to maintain their own privileged position" (86). In this caveat, the rejection of the Western model was not equivalent to the rejection of inter-cultural enrichment, nor was it an endorsement of traditionalism and conservative, repressive elements of a society.
3. Therefore, "total autarchy as a cultural policy is unrealistic and self-denying." Nevertheless, a nondominating policy would have to be alert to current "technico-material realities" (87) in the world system and exercise "informed selectivity" of media technology and cultural products.
4. Selectivity cannot completely bar all efforts of cultural penetration from the dominating sectors. In this situation, alternative policy has to make provisions for widely available informational resources that provide a class perspective for the historical reinterpretation of imported/inserted materials. Culture is not a museum in which traditions are preserved against cultural imperialism. Historical memory must be refreshed so that past experiences, distorted by the dominating groups in order to protect their positions, can be reinterpreted and mind management rendered harmless. This is the vigilance against forgetting that has been a key to understanding Schiller's writings.
5. "Just as cultural autarchy cannot by itself be productive, indiscriminate rejection of technology is an admission of helplessness and discouragement. What is required is the recognition, throughout the decision-making sector, that *technology is a social construct*" (89).
6. Language will be central to policy. A non-dominating policy is alert to definitional power. Dominating languages and forms of expression can perpetuate negative national self-perceptions—harmful racist and gendered meanings as well as dominating colonial language forms will eventually fade from use.
7. Policy can reinforce non-dominating definitional efforts, provided that informational resources are available to help people recognize false labeling and enable them to deconstruct propaganda of the dominating sectors which, for example, calls bombs "peace-keepers," multinational corporations "global citizens," or cultural policy "prior censorship" and so on. This suggests a public informational environment with

vigilant checks and corrections of what George Orwell termed "double-speak" and "news-speak."

8. News can be a liberating consciousness-shaping process when at least two conditions are present: 1) that journalists and media workers make the understanding of liberation movements worldwide a top priority, relating the stories and strategies of resistance to all forms of oppression, cultural, informational, political, etc; 2) news can only do this if it is not presented in "fragmented, minute, anti-historical accounts" that typify the professional commercial broadcasting systems (91).

9. It follows that knowledge workers are recognized as important contributors to non-dominating communications, so assuring working conditions appropriate for a liberating consciousness process is important. The majority of those affected adversely by *institutionalized communication domination* will seek collective influence in the workplace, while a fraction of them will instead identify with the dominating groups and seek privileges accorded to a small professionalized specialist corps. The former group seeking greater participation generates critiques of the system and destroys the *myth of objectivity*; the latter group remains as the talking heads of the dominating communication system.

10. Dominating communications might therefore be sustained by this elite group, so participatory and diverse informational sources would have to persistently refute the legitimacy of this specialized corps of system-serving knowledge "professionals." The legitimacy of professionalized information workers (journalists, managers, experts, pundits, bureaucrats of all sorts) is a sham perpetrated by their false appearance as purveyors of informational pluralism and transparency (*CCD*, 85–94).

In the afterword to *Communication and Cultural Domination* (98–109), Schiller provided a final example concerning the vulnerability of some types of alternative communication policy. Here his target was reformist policy. He argued that a policy that does not seek fundamental change in the power structure was prone to failure (with success measured by the degree of information equality and progressive culture-communications achieved). To show how fragile reformism would be, Schiller turned to the example of communication policy in Chile under the Popular Unity government (1971–1973), which had attempted to implement a pluralistic model of national culture-communication. Such a model depended on the harmonious balance of sociopolitical interests within a single national communications system. Here was an instance in which free enterprise and the "free flow" idea were embodied in a national communications policy. Moreover, as Schiller emphasized, the Chilean model was truly open to a diversity of political and class interests because it secured places within the system for commercial as well as noncommercial, communist, socialist, and educational media organizations, among others. However, Schiller also noted that the reformist policy was predicated on the idea that the pluralization of the system would somehow do away with class conflict as a structuring force. Schiller observed that this was, in practice, not the case.

To show this, Schiller assessed the stated preferences and values of the groups defending private property-holding communications businesses—Chilean media conglomerates with close ties both to the Chilean industrial elites, whose holdings had been nationalized, and to U.S. military-corporate interests. All the evidence indicated that for the capitalist grouping, the existence of a socialist rival within the public sphere could not be tolerated. The socialist and communist media offered programming that raised awareness of class domination and its relation to private business. Moreover, he said, the fundamental difference between the public's attraction to socialist media content and the popularity of the commercial offerings could not be stressed enough—the former derived directly from the political interests of the dominated classes of workers and peasants while the latter derived from dominant interests and functioned primarily to extract as much profit from the dominated classes as possible. As these tensions worsened, the reaction of Chilean businesses and commercial media, with the help of the American military and CIA, led finally to the coup d'etat on September 11, 1973, and the end of this experiment in pluralism. Schiller did not explain this as a theoretical problem but rather drew on the Chilean experience to raise the practical political question about the limits within a class system of a pluralistic cultural and communications policy.

This interpretation of the Chilean struggle informed his thinking about the difficulties ahead for other nations and social movements seeking an alternative path to culture-communications policy. More importantly, perhaps, it helped him reiterate his position that a "communications/cultural policy is national only in its immediate locus of activity, which conforms to the geographic boundaries of the nation. In its essence," Schiller wrote, "it is profoundly international." It is international not only because the forces in conflict are international, but because the vision of a nondominating national policy "recognizes, respects, and desires to enhance people's liberation efforts to achieve critical consciousness wherever they are undertaken" (*CCD*, 91).

In the last pages of his last book, Schiller gathered hopeful signs to imagine history tilting toward democratic renewal and the beginning of the eradication of the "have not" condition. He wondered again what historical role Americans would play in this process as the "cocoon of indifference and self-satisfaction of the country's large middle class [begins] to unspool." It is possible, he suggests, that

> In a time of national adversity, especially when it is unevenly experienced, questioning, tension, and struggle cannot be contained—certainly not by routine political process. In such a time of ferment, the creative energies of the population are bound to be stimulated. This does not mean that the energy automatically will flow in socially positive directions—but flow it will, and its direction will be determined partly by the public's perceived needs and partly by the strength of participants in the social arena. In short, social conflict, embellished with class, racial, ethnic, and gender

features, will reemerge. Undoubtedly, this will be disappointing to dominant social science, which long ago wrote off class struggle as obsolete. No matter . . .

As Numero Uno meets hard times, new ideas, new creativity, new social directions, and new institutional forms, though hardly certainties, may celebrate the next national historical turn. This is a hopeful scenario. The alternative, a repressive state run mainly in the interests of the well-off classes, is not precluded. It would be a national and international disaster. (*Living in the Number One Country*, 200–201)

Herbert Schiller passed away on January 29, 2000, after having spent most of his eighty years of life striving with hope, vitality, and humor to realize the promise of progressive social change. This book has attempted to honor that life, mindful of the ways his work and political commitments were rooted in the historical struggles of the twentieth century. Our inheritance of many of those same struggles ensures that Schiller's ideas and research will continue to be relevant for critical communication studies in the years ahead.

NOTES

1. IRAC members in 2002: National Telecommunications and Information Administration—chairmanship, Department of Agriculture, Department of the Air Force, Department of the Army, Broadcasting Board of Governors, Coast Guard, Department of Commerce, Department of Energy, Federal Emergency Management Agency, General Services Administration, Department of Health and Human Services, Department of the Interior, Department of Justice, National Aeronautics and Space Administration, National Science Foundation, Department of the Navy, Department of State, Department of the Treasury, United States Postal Service, Department of Veterans Affairs, Defense Information Systems Agency—observer, National Communications System—observer, Office of the Assistant Secretary of Defense (C3I)—observer.

2. According to a *Harper's Magazine* investigation written by David Armstrong (2002), President Bush's 2002 *National Security Strategy* did not originate in response to terrorism or the attacks of September 11, but was outlined as Defense Planning Guidance (DPG) for the Pentagon in the early 1990s by Dick Cheney, Colin Powell, and Paul Wolfowitz (at the time Defense Secretary, Chairman of the Joint Chiefs of Staff, and Undersecretary of Defense, respectively). The DPG resurfaced in 2000 as the framework for a report entitled, "Rebuilding America's Defenses: Strategy, Forces, and Resources for a New Century." The report was issued by The Project for the New American Century, a right-wing "educational organization" founded by the neo-conservative writer-publisher William Kristol (members have included, Rumsfeld, Cheney, and Wolfowitz) (www.newamericancentury.org). The authors of the report add an eerie prediction when they lament that "the process of transformation [of the military-industrial complex], even if it brings revolutionary change, is likely to be a long one, absent some catastrophic and catalyzing event—like a new Pearl Harbor" ("Rebuilding America's Defenses," 51).

3. PCIPB board members: Secretary of State; Secretary of the Treasury; Secretary of

Defense; Attorney General; Secretary of Commerce; Secretary of Health and Human Services; Secretary of Transportation; Secretary of Energy; Director of Central Intelligence; Chairman of the Joint Chiefs of Staff; Director of the Federal Emergency Management Agency; Administrator of General Services; Director of the Office of Management and Budget; Director of the Office of Science and Technology Policy; Chief of Staff to the Vice President; Director of the National Economic Council; Assistant to the President for National Security Affairs; Assistant to the President for Homeland Security; Chief of Staff to the President; Director, Critical Infrastructure Assurance Office, Department of Commerce; Manager, National Communications System; Vice Chair, Chief Information Officers' (CIO) Council; Information Assurance Director, National Security Agency; Deputy Director of Central Intelligence for Community Management; Director, National Infrastructure Protection Center, Federal Bureau of Investigation; Department of Justice; FCC representative; other executive branch officials designated by the president.

4. NRIC Member List 2002: Alcatel, Allegiance Telcom, Inc., Alliance for Telecommunications Industry Solutions (ATIS), ALLTEL, AOL-Time Warner, Association of Public Safety—Communications Officials (APCO), AT&T, AT&T Wireless, BellSouth Communications, BITS, Boeing Company Cable & Wireless, Century Telephone, Cingular Wireless, Cisco Systems, Citizens Utilities Comcast Corporation, Communications Cox, Commerce Department's Communications Critical Infrastructure Assurance Office (CIAO), Communications Workers of America, Covad, EarthLink,e-Commerce & Telecommunications, Ericsson, Focal Communications, Genuity, Intelsat, Juniper Networks, Level 3 Communications Inc., Lockheed Martin, Lucent Technologies, Marconi Corporation, Microsoft Corporation, Motorola, National Association of Regulatory and Utility National Communications Systems, National Emergency Number Association (NENA), National Science Foundation, Nextel Communications Inc., Nokia Inc., Nortel Networks, NTIA, Office of Science and Telecommunications Policy, Public Safety Wireless Networks, Qwest, Sprint Corporation, Telcordia Technologies, VeriSign, Verizon Communications, VoiceStream, and WorldCom Inc.

5. By the year 2000, obligatory work of Americans averaged 2000 hours annually, an increase without relief since the 1970s (International Labour Office 1999, 166). On average 12 to 14 percent of the total population in the U.S. lives in poverty, while two-thirds can be considered working class. Moreover, 75 percent of Americans are exposed to the statistical risk that within a ten-year cycle they could be one of the "40 percent of Americans who experience poverty for at least one year" (Zweig 2002, B9). The class tensions in the United States reflect worldwide trends: the richest 20 percent of the world's people earned seventy-four times the amount of the world's poorest in 1997, up from sixty times in 1990 and thirty times in 1960 (UNDP 1999, 3).

Herbert I. Schiller: Publications, 1955–2000

BOOKS

Mass Communications and American Empire. New York: Augustus M. Kelley, 1969. 170 pp. Paperback ed., Beacon Press, 1971; new ed., Westview, 1992.

The Mind Managers. Boston: Beacon Press, 1973. 214 pp. Paperback ed., 1974.

Communication and Cultural Domination. New York: International Arts and Sciences Press, 1976. 126 pp. Paperback ed., M. E. Sharpe, 1977, 1984.

Who Knows: Information in the Age of the Fortune 500. Norwood, N.J.: Ablex (Greenwood Pub.), 1981. 187 pp. Paperback ed. 1982. Chapter entitled "The Privatization of Information" reprinted in *Mass Communication Review Yearbook,* vol. 4, edited by E. Wartella and D. Charles Whitney, pp. 537–68. Beverly Hills, Calif.: Sage, 1983.

Information and the Crisis Economy. Norwood, N.J.: Ablex (Greenwood Pub.), 1984. 133 pp. Paperback ed., Oxford University Press, 1986.

Culture Inc: The Corporate Takeover of Public Expression. New York: Oxford University Press, 1989. 201 pp. Paperback ed., Oxford University Press, 1991.

Information Inequality: The Deepening Social Crisis in America. 157 pp. New York: Routledge, 1996.

Living in the Number One Country: Reflections from a Critic of American Empire. New York: Seven Stories Press, 2000.

COAUTHORED AND COEDITED BOOKS

Super-State: Readings in the Military-Industrial Complex. With Joseph Dexter Phillips. Urbana: University of Illinois Press, 1970. 353 pp. Paperback ed., 1972.

National Sovereignty and International Communication. Edited with Kaarle Nordenstreng. Norwood, N.J.: Ablex (Greenwood Pub.), 1979. 286 pp.

Hope and Folly: The U.S. and UNESCO, 1949–1985. With Edward Herman and William Preston Jr.. Minneapolis: University of Minnesota Press, 1989.

The Ideology of International Communication. With Laurien Alexandre, Robin Anderson, Eileen Mahoney, William Preston Jr., and Colleen Roach. Edited by Laurien Alexandre. New York: Institute for Media Analysis, 1992.

Triumph of the Image: The Media's War in the Persian Gulf—A Global Perspective. Edited with George Gerbner and Hamid Mowlana. Boulder, Colo.: Westview Press, 1992.

Beyond National Sovereignty: International Communication in the 1990s. Edited with Kaarle Nordenstreng. Norwood, N.J.: Ablex (Greenwood Pub.), 1993.

Invisible Crisis: What Conglomerate Control of Media Means for America and the World. Edited with George Gerbner and Hamid Mowlana. Boulder, Colo.: Westview Press, 1996.

ARTICLES, BOOK CHAPTERS, AND OTHER PUBLICATIONS

"Some Effects of the Cold War on United States Foreign Trade." *Review of Economics and Statistics* (November 1955): 428–30.

"Economic Factors in Anti-Americanism in Great Britain Since World War II." *Social Science* (January 1956): 36–42.

"The Adequacy of Raw Materials." *Illinois Business Review* 18, 8 (September 1961).

"The United States and the Educational Needs of the Developing Economies." *Quarterly Review of Economics and Business* 2, 1 (February 1962): 31–38.

"The First Kennedy Budget." *Illinois Business Review* 19, 3 (March 1962).

"The American Right-Wing and the United Nations." *Les Cahiers de la Republique* 44 (May 1962).

"Review of *American Capital and Canadian Resources.*" *Quarterly Review of Economics and Business* 2 (May 1962).

"Access to Raw Materials." *Bulletin of the Atomic Scientists* (October 1962): 16–19.

"A Natural Resources Policy?" *Illinois Business Review* (October 1963).

"An Inward Look at Foreign Aid." *Challenge* (July 1964): 7–10. Reprinted in *Current* (November 1964), and *Front Lines*, U.S. A.I.D.

"The Natural Resources Base—Where Do We Stand?" *World Politics* (July 1964).

"International Resource Relationships in a Changing World." *Social Research* (Autumn 1964): 280–95.

"Current Problems in Raw Materials Supply." *Land Economics* (November 1964): 361–69.

"The Sovereign State of Comsat." *The Nation* (January 25, 1965).

"Review of *Culture Against Man*, by Jules Henry." *Audio-Visual Communication Review* (Spring 1965): 75–77.

"Review of *Mass Media and National Development*, by Wilbur Schramm." *Audio-Visual Communication Review* 13: 2 (Summer 1965): 205–7.

"America Rules the Air Waves." *The Progressive* 30, 3 (March 1966): 26–29.

"The Dirty Business of School Magazines." *Focus/Midwest* 55, 7–8 (March 1966): 10–13.

"Communications and the Third World" *Illinois Political* 1, 1 (April 1966).

"Communications for the Status Quo." *Focus/Midwest* (May 1966).

"Review of *Studies in a Dying Colonialism*, by Frantz Fanon." *Audio-Visual Communication Review* (Summer 1966).

"News of Last Chance in Space Communications." *Illinois Business Review* (December 1966).

"Introduction" to chapter in *As We Saw the Thirties*, edited by Rita J. Simon, pp. 216–18. Urbana: University of Illinois Press, 1967.

"The Slide to International Violence in the Hungering World." *Bulletin of the Atomic Scientists* (January 1967): 4–6.

"National Development Requires Some Social Distance." *Antioch Review* (Spring 1967): 63–75.

"Review of *World Television*." *Audio-Visual Communication Review* (Spring 1967): 122–24.

"Communications Satellites: A New Institutional Setting." *Bulletin of the Atomic Scientists* (April 1967): 4–8. Reprinted in *Communication Satellites in Political Orbit*, edited by Lloyd D. Musolf, pp. 151–95. San Francisco, Calif.: Chandler, 1968.

"The Increasing Military Influence in the Governmental Sector of Communications in the United States." *Administrative Law Review* 19, 3 (May 1967): 303–18.

"Comment" *Bulletin of the Atomic Scientists* (June 1967): 63–64.

"Economics." In *Good Reading*, edited by J. Sherwood Weber. New York: New American Library, 1968.

"Social Control and Individual Freedom." *Bulletin of the Atomic Scientists* (May 1968): 16–21.

"Review of *The First Freedom*, by Bryce W. Rucker." *The Nation* (June 24, 1968): 835–36.

"Review of *Radio and Television Broadcasting on the European Continent*, by Burton Paulu." *Audio-Visual Communication Review* (Fall 1968): 326–29.

"The Use of American Power in the Post-Colonial World." *Massachusetts Review* (Autumn 1968): 631–50.

Program review of "The National Conventions." *Educational Broadcasting Review* (December 1968).

"International Communications, National Sovereignty and Domestic Insurgency." In *Mass Media and International Understanding*, edited by School of Sociology, Political Science and Journalism, pp. 92–100. Ljubljana: Department of Journalism, School of Sociology, Political Science and Journalism, 1969.

"The Mass Media and the Public Interest." In *Television Today: The End of Communications and the Death of Community*, pp. 53–69. Washington, D.C.: Institute for Policy Studies, 1969.

"Public Education Under Siege." *The Progressive* (May 1969).

"Television Comes to Israel." *Educational Broadcasting Review* 3, 4 (August 1969): 45–52.

"Review of *The Information Machines*, by Ben H. Bagdikian." *Audio-Visual Communication Review* (Autumn 1969): 331–33.

"Review of *Western Economic Warfare 1947–1967. A Case Study of Foreign Policy*, by Gunnar Adler-Carlson." *Bulletin of the Atomic Scientists* (October 1969): 44–46.

"Who Owns the Air." *Comment, the Center Magazine* 3, 3 (May 1970): 90–91.

"Mind Management: Mass Media in the Advanced Industrial State." *Quarterly Review of Economics and Business* (Spring 1971): 39–52. Reprinted in *Mass Media and Society*, by Alan Wells. Palo Alto, Calif.: National Press, 1972.

"Review of *The Adversaries: Politics and the Press*, by William Rivers." *Science and Society* (Spring 1971): 115–17.

"Review of *The Press and the Cold War*, by James Aronson." *Journalism Quarterly* (Spring 1971): 139–41.

"Madison Avenue Imperialism." *Transaction-Society* (March–April 1971): 52–58. Reprinted in *Communications in International Politics*, edited by Richard L. Merritt. Urbana: University of Illinois Press, 1972; also reprinted in *Sociological Realities*, by I. L. Horowitz and C. Nanry. New York: Harper & Row, 1975.

"Review of *The Pentagon Propaganda Machine*, by William Fulbright." *Bulletin of the Atomic Scientists* (April 1971): 43–44.

"Review of *The Age of Imperialism*, by Harry Magdoff." *Journal of Economic History* (June 1971): 507–10.

Guest editorial on *War and Peace and the American University*. *College and University Business* (August 1971): 28–29.

"Review of *Communications and National Integration in Communist China*, by Alan P.L. Liu." *Quarterly Review of Economics and Business* (Autumn 1971): 93–95.

"Chile: An End to Cultural Colonialism." With Dallas Smythe. *Transaction-Society* (March 1972): 35–39.

"Review of *Television, the Business Behind the Box* by Les Brown." *Journalism Quarterly* (Spring 1972): 189–90.

"The Polling Industry: The Measurement and Manufacture of Opinion." *Psychology Today* (July 1972).

"Feedback 4: Broadcast Journalism:" *Performance* 3 (July–August 1972): 57–70.

"Review of *The Public Persuader*." *Journal of Economic Issues* (September 1972): 156–58.

"Review of *Picture Tube Imperialism?* by Alan Wells." *Journalism Quarterly* (Winter 1972–73).

"Review of *The Universal Eye* by Timothy Green." *Journalism Quarterly* (Winter 1972–73).

"Authentic National Development Versus the Free Flow of Information." In *Communication Technology and Social Policy*, edited by George Gerbner, Larry Gross, and William Melody. New York: Wiley Interscience, 1973.

"The Electronic Invaders." *The Progressive* (August 1973). Reprinted as "Satellite Broadcasting and Cultural Imperialism." *Washington Star*, July 29, 1973.

"Mass Communication Research on the Power Structures of Society: A Proposal." In *Mass Media Research*, edited by Cees J. Hamelink, pp. 43–45. Geneva: Lutheran World Federation, 1973.

"Review of *The Politics and Technology of Satellite Communications*." *Journalism Quarterly* (Summer 1973).

"Statement." In *Television Traffic—A One-Way Street?* pp. 49–50. Reports and Papers on Mass Communication No. 70. Paris: UNESCO, 1974.

"Waiting for Orders: Mass Communications Research in the United States." *Gazette* 20, 1 (1974): 11–21.

"Don't Answer That Questionnaire." *Kontext* (Amsterdam) (May 8, 1974): 10–11.

"Review of *The Politics of Communication*, by Claus Mueller." *Journalism Quarterly* (Summer 1974): 348–49.

"The Mechanics of International Cultural Domination." *Le Monde Diplomatique* (December 1974).

"Freedom for the Free Flow of Information." *Journal of Communication* 24, 1 (Winter 1974).

"Genesis of the Free Flow of Information Principle: The Imposition of Communication Domination." *Instant Research on Peace and Violence* (Tampere, Finland) 5, 1 (1975): 75–86. Reprinted in French as "Libre Circulation et Domination Mondiale." *Le Monde Diplomatique* (September 1975): 18–19; in Russian, in *Soviet Russia*, October 17, 1975;

and in *Crisis in International News: Policies and Prospects*, edited by Jim Richstad and Michael Anderson. New York: Columbia University Press, 1981.

"Introduction." Special issue, *Kroniek van Afrika*. Leiden: Afrika-Studien-Centrum, Leiden University, 1975.

"The Material Side of Consciousness." In *Der Anteil der Massenmedien bei der Herausbildung des Bewusstseins in der sich wandelnden Welt*, edited by the International Association for Mass Communication Research, pp. 24–30. Leipzig: Karl Marx Universität, 1975. Reprinted in *The Democratic Journalist* (June 1976); *Journal of the Centre for Advanced TV Studies* (London) (1976).

"The Appearance of National-Communications Policies: A New Arena for Social Struggle." *Gazette* 21, 2 (1975): 82–94.

"The Balance of Power and the Ecology of Ideas." Society for General Systems Research, Annual AAAS meetings, Denver, Colo., February 1975.

"Review of *Who Controls the Mass Media?* by Martin Seiden" *Journal of Communication* (Summer 1975): 206–8.

"Review of *Intelsat: Politics and Functionalism.*" *Journal of Communication* (Winter 1975): 213–17.

"International Advertising and International Communications." *Instant Research on Peace and Violence* 4 (1976).

"Review of *Radio Power*, by Julian Hale." *Journalism Quarterly* (1976).

"Transnational Media and National Development." In *Fair Communication Policy Conference*, edited by Jim Richstad. Honolulu: East-West Center, 1976.

"Fabricated Culture." *Lier en Boog* (Holland) 4 (July 1976).

"An Effort to Achieve a Delicate Balance." Reply to comment on "Helsinki: The New Equation." With Kaarle Nordenstreng. *Journal of Communication* 26, 3 (Summer 1976): 237–38.

"Review of *Captains of Consciousness: The Social Roots of Advertising*, by Stuart Ewen." *Journal of Communication* 26, 4 (Autumn 1976): 227–28.

"Helsinki: The New Equation (On Free Flow of Information)." With Kaarle Nordenstreng. *Journal of Communication* (Winter 1976).

"Mind Managing the Food and Energy Crisis." In *The Political Economy of Food and Energy*, edited by Louis Junker. Michigan Business Papers No. 62, Ann Arbor: University of Michigan, 1977.

"Now: A New International Information Order?" *Intellect* 106, 2386 (August 1977): 42.

"Review of *Mass Media: Systems and Effects*, by W. Phillips Davison and James Boyland." *Contemporary Sociology* (September 1977): 548.

"Who's Managing Your Minds?" Interview with Jack Wintz, O.F.M. *St. Anthony's Messenger* (September 1977): 12–17.

"Review of *The Manipulators*, by Robert Sobel." *Science and Society* 41, 3 (Fall 1977): 346–49.

"Review of *The Media Are American*, by Jeremy Tunstall." *Journal of Communication* 27, 4 (Autumn 1977): 226–29.

"Review of *Media, Politics and Democracy*, by Bernard Rubin, and *Snap, Crackle and Popular Taste*, by Jeffrey Schrank" *The Nation* (October 29, 1977): 439–42.

"Review of *Media World: Programming the Public.*" *Journalism Quarterly* 54, 4 (Winter 1977): 812–13.

"In Search of a New World Information Order." *Baltimore Sun*, December 4, 1977: K-2.

"New Modes of Cultural Domination." *Conradh na Galilge* (Dublin) (1978).

"'Free Communications Under the Re-Write." *Los Angeles Times,* Opinion Section, August 20, 1978.

"Computer Communications for Whom and for What?" *Journal of Communication* 28, 4 (Autumn 1978). Longer version in *Computer World* (February 12, 1979).

"Review of *The Politics of Propaganda: The Office of War Propaganda, 1942–1945,* by Allan M. Winkler." *Journalism Quarterly* 55, 3 (Autumn 1978).

"Decolonization of Information: Steps Toward a New World Information Order." *Latin American Perspectives* 16 (Winter 1978): 35–48.

"U.S. Information Policy After Nairobi." *Le Monde Diplomatique* (March 1979). Longer version in English and Spanish published by ILET (Latin American Institute for Transnational Studies), September 1979.

"Media and Imperialism." *Revue Française d'Etudes Americaines* (Paris) (October 1978). Reprinted in *Tabloid* (November 1979).

"Transnational Business, the Free Flow of Information, and the Question of Regulation." In *Telecommunications Policy and the Citizen,* edited by Tim Haight. New York: Praeger, 1979.

"The Transnational Corporation and the International Flow of Information." *Current Research on Peace and Violence* (Tampere) (1979).

"Communication Accompanies Capital Flows." In International Commission for the Study of Communication Problems, The MacBride Commission. Paris: UNESCO, May 1979.

"Resistances a la Suprematie Americaine dans le Domaine de l'Information." *Communication et Information* 3, 1 (1979).

"Review of *The Sponsor,* by Erik Barnouw." *Journal of Communication* 29, 1 (Winter 1979).

"Free Flow and Regulation." *Follies: A Journal of the Arts and Opinion* (December 1979).

"Electronic Utopias and Structural Realities." In *A Reader on the MacBride Report,* edited by Cees Hamelink. Rome: IDOC, 1980. Reprinted in *Mass Communication Review Yearbook,* vol. 3. Beverly Hills, Calif.: Sage, 1982.

"Whose New International Economic and Information Order?" *Communication* 5, 4 (1980): 299–314.

"Will Advanced Communication Technology Create a New International Information Order?" *WACC Journal* 27, 4 (1980). Reprinted in *Media Information Australia* (February 1981).

"Communications in the 1980s: A Global Perspective." *Equal Opportunity Forum* (January 1980): 18–19.

"Review of *Friendly Fascism* by Bertram Gross." *Journal of Communication* 30, 4 (Autumn 1980): 194–98.

"Transnational Communication and Self-Reliance." *Third World* (Mexico) (November–December 1980): 64–66.

"Foreword." In *Dependency Road* by Dallas W. Smythe. Norwood, N.J.: Ablex (Greenwood Pub.), 1981.

"The Free Flow Doctrine: Will It last Into the 21st Century?" In *Communications in the 21st Century,* edited by R. W. Haigh, George Gerbner, and R. B. Byrne. New York. Wiley, 1981.

"The War of Words Heats Up." *In These Times* (March 4–10, 1981).

"Information for What Kind of a Society?" Edward R. Morrow Symposium, Washington State University, April 17, 1981. Reprinted in *Telecommunication Issues*, edited by J. Salvaggio. New York: Longman, 1983; *Current Research on Peace and Violence* (March 1981).

"Perspectives on Communication Research: An Exchange." *Journal of Communication* 31, 3 (Summer 1981): 15–23.

"The Diplomacy of Cultural Domination and the Free Flow of Information." *Freedomways* 22, 3 (1982): 144–62.

"The Privatizing of Information: Who Can Own What America Knows?" With Anita Schiller. *The Nation* (April 17, 1982): 461–63. Received 1982 Gold PEN Award for magazine writing. Los Angeles PEN Center, May 28, 1982.

"Information: America's New Global Empire." *Channels of Communication* (September 1982): 30–33. Reprinted in *Global Issues* annual edition, edited by Robert Jackson, 1985.

"Foreword." In *Cultural Autonomy in Global Communications*, by Cees Hamelink. New York: Longman, 1983.

"The Communication Revolution: Who Benefits?" *Media Development* 30 (1983): 18–21.

"New Technologies of Communication." *Chasqui* 6 (January–June 1983): 46–53.

"Review of *To Inform or to Control* by Oswald Ganley and Gladys Ganley." *Journal of Communication* 33, 2 (Spring 1983): 182–44.

"The World Crisis and the New Information Technologies." *Columbia Journal of World Business* 18, 1 (Spring 1983).

"Critical Research in the Information Age." *Journal of Communication* 33, 3 (Summer 1983): 249–57.

"The Language of Science and Science of Domination." *Enjeu* 40 (October 1983): 39–41.

"Information: America's New Global Empire." *Transnational Data Report* 6, 7 (October–November 1983): 360–61.

"Corrientes de Información Electrónica y el Creciente Ataque a la Soberanía Nacional." In *Video, Cultura Nacional y Subdesarrollo*, pp. 125–37. Havana, 1984.

"Informatics and Information Flows: The Underpinnings of Transnational Capitalism." In *Critical Communication Review* 2, edited by Vincent Mosco and Janet Wasko. Norwood, N.J.: Ablex (Greenwood Pub.), 1984.

"Remote Sensing by Satellite: Global Hegemony or Social Utility." In *World Communications: A Handbook*, edited by George Gerbner and Marsha Siefert. New York: Longman, 1984.

"L'Atout Informatique: Des Trusts a L'Assaut du Ciel." *Le Monde Diplomatique* (March 1984): 6–7.

"Scrapping the International System: The U.S. Withdrawal from UNESCO." *Journal of Communication* 34: 4 (Fall 1984).

"New Information Technologies and Old Objectives." *Science and Public Policy* 1, 6 (December 1984): 382–83.

"Beneficiaries and Victims of the Information Age: The Systematic Diminution of the Public's Supply of Meaningful Information." *Vision and Reality*, special edition of *Papers in Comparative Studies* 4 (1985): 185–92.

"Electronic Information Flows: New Basis for Global Domination?" In *Television in Transition*, edited by Richard Collins, Phillip Drummond, and Richard Paterson. London: British Film Institute, 1985.

"Expanding the Club-New Vistas for TDF." In *International Information Economy Handbook*, edited by G. Russell Pipe and Chris Brown, pp. 31–32. Springfield, Va.: Transnational Data Reporting Service, 1985.

"Privatizing the Public Sector: The Information Connection." *Information and Behavior* 1, 1 (1985).

"Behind the Media Merger Movement." *The Nation* (June 8, 1985): 696–98. Reprinted in the *Cleveland Plain-Dealer* (June 23, 1985).

"Breaking the West's Media Monopoly: The U.N. and Information." *The Nation* (September 21, 1985): 248–51.

"Review of *Keeping America Uninformed: Government Secrecy in the 1980's,* by Donna Demac." *Telecommunications Policy* (September 1985).

"Review of *The New Politics of Science,* by David Dickson." *Journal of Communication* 35, 1 (Winter 1985): 194–96.

"Information—A Shrinking Resource." *The Nation* (December 28, 1985–January 4, 1986): 708–10.

"Democracy in an Information Society." Comment on article by Theodore Sterling. *The Information Society* 4, 1 & 2 (1986): 123–26.

"The Erosion of National Sovereignty by the World Business System." In *The Myth of the Information Revolution,* edited by Michael Traber, pp. 21–34. London: Sage, 1986.

"Strengths and Weaknesses of the New International Information Empire!" In *Communication for All,* edited by Philip Lee, 17–32. Maryknoll, N.Y.: Orbis, 1986.

"Review of *Television and the Red Menace: The Video Road to Vietnam,* edited by J. Fred McDonald." *Contemporary Sociology* 15, 1 (January 1986): 77–79.

"Commercializing Information." With Anita R. Schiller. *The Nation* (October 4, 1986): 306–9.

"The New Information Technologies: New Means of Creating Cultural Dependency?" In *Dependency Issues in Korean Development,* edited by Kyong Dong Kim. Seoul: Seoul National University Press, 1987.

"Old Foundations for a New (Information) Age." In *Competing Visions, Complex Realities.* Edited by Jorge Reina Schement and Leah Lievrouw, pp. 23–31. Norwood, N.J.: Ablex (Greenwood Pub.), 1987.

"Review of *Exporting the First Amendment: The Press-Government Crusade of 1945–1952,* by Margaret A. Blanchard." *Journal of Communication* (Summer 1987): 155–60.

"Information: Important Issue for '88" *The Nation* (July 4–11, 1987): 1,6.

Excerpt from *Who Knows.* In *Questioning Technology,* edited by John Zerzan and Alice Carnes, pp. 170–76. London: Freedom Press, 1988.

"Libraries, Public Access to Information and Commerce." With Anita R. Schiller. In *The Political Economy of Information,* edited by Vincent Mosco and Janet Wasko, pp. 146–66. Madison: University of Wisconsin Press, 1988.

"Preface." In *The Hidden War of Information,* by Enrique Gonzalez-Manet. Translated by Laurien Alexandre. Norwood, N.J.: Ablex (Greenwood Pub.), 1988.

"Corporate Speech, Power Politics and the First Amendment." *The Independent* (July 1988): 10–13.

"Vers un nouveau siècle d'imperialisme americain." *Le Monde diplomatique* (Aout 1988): 1, 18–19.

"Computers and the World Economy." In *The Encyclopedia of Communications.* New York: Oxford University Press, 1989.

"The Privatization of Culture." In *Cultural Politics in Contemporary America*, edited by Sut Jhally and Ian Angus, pp. 317–32. New York: Routledge, 1989.

"Pitchers at an Exhibition: Corporate Sponsorship of Museums." *The Nation* 249 (July 10 1989): 37+

"Review of *Freedom of Speech on Private Property* by Warren Freedman." *Journal of Communication* 39 (Autumn 1989): 65–67.

"Review of *United States and the Direct Broadcast Satellite*, by Sarah Fletcher Luther." *Socialism and Democracy* (Spring–Summer 1989): 236–39.

"Communication of Knowledge in an Information Society." With Bernard Miège. In *The Information Society: Evolving Landscapes*, edited by Jacques Berleur, Andrew Clement, Richard Sizer, and Diane Whitehouse, pp. 161–67. New York: Springer, 1990.

"Forgetful and Short-Sighted—What Hope for the Future." *Media Development* 3 (1990): 26–27.

"Kultursponsoring in den USA." *Media Perspektiven* 11 (1990): 730–36.

"Review of *Global Television* by Cynthia Schneider and Brian Wallis." *Art in America* 78 (Jan. 1990): 41+

"Television Is a Social—Not a Biological or Technological—Problem." Comment on article, "The First Amendment in an Age of Paratroopers." *Texas Law Review* 68, 6 (May 1990): 1169–78.

"Democratic Illusions." *Multinational Monitor* 11, 6 (June 1990): 19–22.

"Sayonara MCA." *The Nation* (December 31, 1990): 828–29.

"The Global Commercialization of Culture." *The Progressive Librarian* 2 (Winter 1990–1991): 15–22.

"Gulf War Forum Interviews." *Propaganda Review* 7 (1991).

"An Interview with Herbert I. Schiller." (Lai-si Tsui). *Media Development* 27, 1 (1991): 50–52.

"My Graduate Education (1946–1948), Sponsored by the U.S. Military Government of Germany." In *Medien/Kultur*, edited by Knot Hickethier and Siegfried Zielinski, pp. 23–29. Berlin: Volker Spiess, 1991.

"Public Information Goes Corporate." *Library Journal* 116, 6 (1991): 42–45.

"Le Citoyen sous le Rouleau Compresseur des Fimes de la Communication." *Le Monde Diplomatique* (February 1991): 26–27.

"Whose New World Order?" *Lies of Our Times* (February 1991): 12–13.

"Not Yet a Post-Imperialist Era." *Critical Studies in Mass Communication* 8, 1 (March 1991): 13–28.

"Manipuler et Controler les Coeurs et les Esprits." *Le Monde Diplomatique* (May 1991): 14–15.

"Nuestros Medios de Comunicación Parecen Apéndices del Pentágono." *El Independiente* (Madrid) (May 26, 1991): 40–41.

"Read This." (Deborah Baldwin). *Common Cause Magazine* (May–June 1991): 30–36.

"Corporate Sponsorship: Institutionalized Censorship of the Cultural Realm." *Art Journal* (Fall 1991).

"Anticipating the Next Radical Moment: An Unexpected Locale." In *Illuminating the Blindspots: Essays in Honor of Dallas Smythe*. Edited by Janet Wasko, Vincent Mosco, and Manjunath Pendakur. Norwood, N.J.: Ablex (Greenwood Pub.), 1993.

"Highway Robbers" (editorial). *The Nation* 257, 21 (1993): 753.

"The Information Highway: Public Way or Private Road." *The Nation* 257, 2 (1993): 64–66.

"Transnational Media: Creating Consumers Worldwide." *Journal of International Affairs* 47 (Summer 1993): 47–58.

"Communication, Technology and Ecology." In *Mass Communication Research: On Problem and Policies*, edited by Cees J. Hamelink and Olga Linné. Norwood, N.J.: Ablex (Greenwood Pub.), 1994.

"Foreword." In *Networks of Power: Corporate TV's Threat to Democracy* by Dennis W. Mazzocco. South End Press, 1994.

"Media, Technology, and the Market: The Interacting Dynamic." In Gretchen Bender and Timothy Druckrey, *Culture on the Brink: Ideologies of Technology.* Seattle: Bay Press 1994, 41–46.

"Foreword." In *Propaganda Inc.: Selling America's Culture to the World* by Nancy Snow. New York: Seven Stories Press, 1998.

"Striving for Communication Dominance: A Half Century Review." In *Electronic Empires: Global Media and Local Resistance.* Edited by D. K. Thussu, pp. 17–26. London: Arnold, 1998.

"Décervelage à l'Americaine." *Le Monde Diplomatique* (August 1999): 15.

"Digitised Capitalism: What has Changed?" In *Media Power, Professionals and Policies.* Edited by H. Tumber, pp. 116–26. London, Routledge, 2000.

"The Social Context of Research and Theory." In *Consuming Audiences? Production and Reception in Media Research.* Edited by Ingunn Hagen and Janet Wasko. Cresskill, N.J.: Hampton Press, 2000.

References

Armstrong, David. 2002. "Dick Cheney's Song of America: Drafting a Plan for Global Dominance." *Harper's Magazine*, October, 76–83.

Barnouw, Erik. 1966. *A History of Broadcasting in the United States, Volume 1: A Tower of Babel. To 1933*. London: Oxford University Press.

Becker, Jörg, Göran Hedebro, and Leena Paldán. 1986. *Communication and Domination: Essays to Honor Herbert I. Schiller*. Norwood, N.J.: Ablex Publishing Corporation.

Borger, Julian, and David Teather. 2003. "So much for the peace dividend: Pentagon is winning the battle for a $400bn budget." *The Guardian*. May 22. www.guardian.co.uk/usa/story/0,12271,960922,00.html (accessed May 22, 2003).

Calvo, Dana. 2001. "Hollywood Signs on to Assist War Effort." *The Los Angeles Times*, November 12.

Cecil, Matthew. 2002. "Press Every Angle: FBI Public Relations and the 'Smear Campaign' of 1958." *American Journalism* 19 (Winter): 39–58.

Center for Defense Information. 2002. *2001–2002 Military Almanac*. Washington D.C., at www.cdi.org/issues/usmi (accessed March 5, 2003).

Day, Gary. 2002. "Freedoms Threatened—Let's Go Shopping." *The Times Higher Education Supplement* (July 19): 24.

Fairness and Accuracy in Reporting. 2001a. "Civilian Casualties Not News." November 8, at www.fair.org (accessed November 12, 2001).

———. 2001b. "Networks Accept Government Guidance." October 12, at www.fair.org (accessed November 12, 2001).

———. 2003. "In Iraq Crisis, Networks Are Megaphones for Official Views." March 18, at www.fair.org/reports/iraq-sources.html (accessed March 19, 2003).

Freedland, Jonathan. 2002. "Rome, AD . . . Rome, DC?" *The Guardian*, September 18, at www.guardian.co.uk/usa/story/0,12271,794163,00.html (accessed January 8, 2003).

Gandy, Oscar H., Jr. 1993. *The Panoptic Sort: A Political Economy of Personal Information*. Boulder, Colo.: Westview Press.

Gribble, Joanne. 2000. "Forty Years of UCSD Perspective." *San Diego Metropolitan Uptown Examiner & Daily Business Report* 15, 12 (September): 34–36.

Guback, Thomas. 1969. *The International Film Industry: Western Europe and America Since 1945*. Bloomington: Indiana University Press.

————. 1994. *Counterclockwise: Perspectives on Communication: Dallas Smythe.* Boulder, Colo.: Westview Press.

Hamelink, Cees. 1983. *Cultural Autonomy in Global Communications.* London: Longman.

————. 2001. "Remembering Herbert Schiller: Our Common Efforts." *Television and New Media* 2, 1: 11–16.

Herman, Edward. 1990. "Media in the U.S. Political Economy." In Downing et al., *Questioning the Media.* Thousand Oaks, Calif.: Sage Publications.

————. 2002. "Remembering Herbert Schiller." *Dollars & Sense* 2 (March).

Hitchens, Christopher. 2001. *The Trial of Henry Kissinger.* London: Verso Books.

Hobsbawm, Eric J. 1992. *Nations and Nationalism since 1780: Programme, Myth, Reality.* 2d edition. Cambridge: Cambridge University Press.

International Labour Office. 1999. *Key Indicators of the Labor Market.* Geneva.

Kanellos, Michael. 2002. "One Billion PCs Shipped since the Altair." Zdnet, July 1. zdnet .com.com/2100–1103–940783.html (accessed August 10, 2002).

Kindleberger, Charles P. 1973. "Oral History Interview with Charles P. Kindleberger," by Richard D. McKinzie. Cambridge, Massachusetts, July 16. Truman Library, at www. trumanlibrary.org/oralhist/kindbrgr.htm (accessed August 15, 2002).

Kleinwächter, Wolfgang. 1995. "Justice, Equality, and Professional Ethics in Journalism: Kaarle Nordenstreng's Actions and Reflections." In John Lent, ed. *A Different Road Taken: Profiles in Critical Communication.* Boulder, Colo.: Westview Press, 243–55.

Koger, Dave, and Rebecca L. Dodge. 1998. "Geosat Starts Up R&D on Exploration Sensor." *Oil & Gas Journal* (October 5): 113.

Landis, Fred. 1975. "Psychological Warfare in Chile: The CIA Makes Headlines." *Liberation* 19 (March–April): 21–32.

Lent, John. 1995. *A Different Road Taken: Profiles in Critical Communication.* Boulder, Colo.: Westview.

————. 2001. "Personal Recollections of Herb Schiller." *Television and New Media* 2, 1: 39–41.

Lewis, Justin. 2001. *Constructing Public Opinion: How Political Elites Do What They Like and Why We Seem to Go along with It.* New York: Columbia University Press.

Markoff, John. 2003. "Experts Say Technology is Widely Disseminated Inside and Outside Military." *The New York Times,* May 21, A20.

Mattelart, Armand. 1991. *Advertising International: The Privatization of Public Space.* Translated by Michael Chanan. London: Comedia/Routledge.

Mayle, Adam, and Alex Knott. 2002. "Outsourcing Big Brother: Office of Total Information Awareness Relies on Private Sector to Track Americans." Center for Public Integrity, December 17, at www.public-i.org/dtaweb/report.asp?ReportID = 484 (accessed January, 16, 2003).

McChesney, Robert W. 1996. "Is There Any Hope for Cultural Studies?" *Monthly Review* 47, 10 (March): 1–18.

————. 1999. *Rich Media, Poor Democracy: Communication Politics in Dubious Times.* Urbana: University of Illinois Press.

Memorandum from OMB Director Mitchell E. Daniels Jr. to Heads of Executive Departments and Agencies, May 3, 2002.

Miller, Judith. 2002. "Report Calls for Plan of Sharing Data to Prevent Terror." *New York Times,* October 7, A11.

Miller, Toby, Nitin Govil, John McMurria, and Richard Maxwell. 2001. *Global Hollywood*. London: British Film Institute.

Mills, C. Wright. 1956. *The Power Elite*. London: Oxford University Press.

Morley, David. 1993. *Television, Audiences, and Cultural Studies*. London: Routledge.

Mosco, Vincent. 1996. *The Political Economy Of Communication: Rethinking and Renewal*. London, Thousand Oaks, Calif., and New Delhi: Sage Publications.

———. 2001a. "Living On in the Number One Country: The Legacy of Herbert I. Schiller." *Journal of Broadcasting and Electronic Media* 45 (Winter): 191.

———. 2001b. "Herbert Schiller." *Television and New Media* 2 (February): 27–30.

Mowlana, Hamid. 2001. "Remembering Herbert I. Schiller." *Television and New Media* 2, 1 (February): 19–26.

Nordenstreng, Kaarle. 1968. "Communication Research in the U.S.: A Critical perspective." *Gazette* 14: 207–16.

———. 1993. "New Information Order and Communication Scholarship: Reflections on a Delicate Relationship." In Janet Wasko, Vincent Mosco, and Manjunath Pendakur, editors, *Illuminating the Blindspots: Essays Honoring Dallas W. Smythe*. Norwood, N.J.: Ablex Publishing Corporation, 251–73.

Nordenstreng, Kaarle, and Tapio Varis. 1974. *Television Traffic—One Way Street? A Survey and Analysis of the International Flow of Television Programme Material*. Reports and Papers on Mass Communication, no. 70. Paris: UNESCO.

Pendakur, Manjunath. 2001. "Remembering Herb Schiller." In *Television and New Media* 2, 1 (February): 43–44.

Phillips, Peter, ed. 2002. *Censored 2003: The Top 25 Censored Stories of 2001–2002*. New York: Seven Stories Press.

Postrel, V. 1999. "The Pleasures of Persuasion." *Wall Street Journal*, August 2.

Risen, James, and Thom Shanker. 2002. "Rumsfeld Moves to Strengthen His Grip on Military Intelligence." *New York Times*, August 3, A1.

Ross, Andrew. 1997. *No Sweat: Fashion, Free Trade, and the Rights of Garment Workers*. London: Verso.

Schiller, Herbert, and Dallas Smythe. 1972. "Chile: An End to Cultural Colonialism." *Transaction-Society* (March): 35–39, 61.

Senghaas, Dieter. 1980. "Self Reliance and Autocentric Development: Historical Experiences and Contemporary Challenges." *Bulletin of Peace Proposals* 1 (44–51).

Shanker, Thom. 2002. "U.S. Explores a New World of Warfare." *New York Times*, August 20, A8.

Shapiro, Michael. 1997. *Violent Cartographies: Mapping Cultures of War*. Minneapolis: University of Minnesota Press.

Simpson, Christopher. 1994. *Science of Coercion: Communication Research and Psychological Warfare, 1945–1960*. New York: Oxford University Press.

Solomon, Norman. 2001. "War Needs Good Public Relations." *Media Beat*, at www.fair.org/media-beat/011025.html (accessed November 12, 2001).

Sreberny-Mohammadi, Annabelle, and Ali Mohammadi. 1995. *Small Media, Big Revolution*. Minneapolis: University of Minnesota Press.

Tsui, Lai-si. 1995. "Herbert Schiller: Clarion Voice against Cultural Hegemony." In John Lent, *A Different Road Taken: Profiles in Critical Communication*. Boulder, Colo.: Westview Press, 155–72.

UNESCO. 1969. "Meeting of Experts on Mass Communication and Society." Montreal, June 21–30. Paris (COM/MD/8).

United Nations Development Programme. 1999. *Human Development Report.*

United States. *National Security Strategy of the United States of America.* 2002. Washington: President of the United States. September 17. Downloadable PDF at www.whitehouse.gov/nsc/nss.html (accessed January 23, 2003).

"U.S. Military Bases and Empire." 2002. The Editors. *Monthly Review.* March. www.monthlyreview.org/0302editr.htm (accessed May 22, 2003).

"U.S. Military Might: The Facts." 2002. *The Observer* (Guardian Newspapers Ltd). March 10. www.observer.co.uk/waronterrorism/story/0,1373,665108,00.html (accessed May 22, 2003).

Van Dinh, Tran. 1979. "Nonalignment and Cultural Imperialism." In Kaarle Nordenstreng and Herbert I. Schiller, *National Sovereignty and International Communication.* Norwood, N.J.: Ablex Publishing Corporation.

Victory, Nancy J. 2002. "Current and Emerging Solutions to Public Safety Communications." *Interoperability Summit: Creating New Opportunities with Technology.* Tuesday, June 11, 2002, Washington, D.C., National Telecommunications and Information Administration.

Webster, Frank. 2001. "Herbert I. Schiller." *Television and New Media* 2, 1 (February): 31–33.

Webster, Frank, and Kevin Robins. 1986. *Information Technology: A Luddite Analysis.* Norwood, N.J.: Ablex Publishing Corporation.

Wyatt, Justin. 1995. *High Concept: Movies and Marketing in Hollywood.* Austin: University of Texas.

Zweig, Michael. 2002. Interview. "Welcome to the Working Class!" *New York Times,* July 13, B9.

Index

About the Author

Richard Maxwell is Professor of Media Studies at Queens College, City University of New York. He is author of *The Spectacle of Democracy: Spanish Television, Nationalism, and Political Transition,* the editor of *Culture Works: The Political Economy of Culture,* and is coauthor of *Global Hollywood.*

DATE DUE

GAYLORD			PRINTED IN U.S.A.